PROFESSIONAL RESOURCES

M000290520

The Four-Blocks™ Literacy Model

THE TEACHER'S GUIDE

TO

BUILDING BLOCKS™

A Developmentally Appropriate, Multilevel Framework
for Kindergarten

by

Dorothy P. Hall

and

Elaine Williams

Editors
Joey Bland
Tracy Soles

Artist
Bill Neville

Cover Design
Mike Duggins

0-88724-580-3

Dedications

This book is dedicated to my mother, Jeanne Parzyk, and my late father, Francis Parzyk, along with my four sisters, Jeanne, Katherine, Frances, and Christine. Also my daughters, Michelle and Suzanne, who have always been a source of encouragement and pride.

I want to thank Pat Cunningham, friend extraordinaire, for telling me it is easier to write about the things you are passionate about, and for then teaching me how to do this.

I want to recognize the kindergarten teachers who have helped with the Building Blocks framework. I have learned so much from watching and teaching in their classes. Especially Elaine Williams and Kim Murph Fansler, who have worked with Wake Forest University student teachers and taught them how to put into practice the things Pat and I preach.

Finally, I want to thank two student teachers, Alison Sigmon and Kelly Simon, who worked under the supervision of Elaine and Kim while I wrote this book. They lived this book by teaching the lessons, reading our drafts, and helping with their comments and suggestions.

Dottie Hall

This book is dedicated to my mother, Mary Williams, and my late father, Smyer Williams; my sisters, Melissa and Laura; and my best friend, Ann Rolfe; who have always listened and loved. Also, my nephews, John and Paul; and my niece, Mary Hannah; as well as my goddaughter, Eleanor Rolfe; and her sisters, Susan and Sally whom I have watched, and learned from, and shared their stories.

I want to thank my friends and mentors Pat Cunningham and Dottie Hall. They have taught me, believed in me, and continue to help me grow as a person and a teacher.

I also want to thank the teachers, principals, and parents I have worked with through the years who have encouraged my journey as a kindergarten teacher.

Last, but not least, I recognize the children I have taught over the years. They have taught me more about <u>life</u> than I have taught them about literacy!

Elaine Williams

TABLE OF CONTENTS

Table of Contents

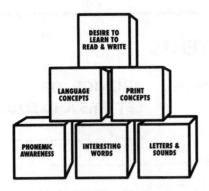

Chapter 1
Introduction

Welcome to the wonderful world of kindergarten! This book is about teaching reading, writing, and phonics in a developmentally appropriate way—not like teachers do in first or second grade, but in a way that is just right for kindergarten kids!

Kindergarten teachers have the responsibility—and the privilege—of introducing young children to school life and literacy. If the introduction is a pleasant one, then the child will develop an attitude toward school and learning which can carry her through the occasionally difficult situations that everyone is bound to meet in the climb up the educational ladder. Most kindergarten children eagerly look forward to starting school. They see themselves as being old enough for "real" school, not day care or "play" school. A few children are upset at the thought of leaving their mothers, but most kindergarten children are proud they have reached this milestone in their lives! Under the guidance of a wise and capable kindergarten teacher, these youngsters are ready for the greatest adventure of their lives—learning to read and write.

Young children see themselves as being capable when they enter school, regardless of their entering literacy level. If you ask a five-year-old, "Can you read?", he will answer, "Yes," as he "pretend reads" his favorite books or stories with lots of expression. If you ask a five-year-old, "Can you write?", he will also answer, "Yes," as he scribbles up and down with his best strokes using his pencils, crayons, or markers. If you ask a five-year-old, "Can you fly?", he will fly around the room with outstretched arms. Five-year-olds can do anything! All five years olds, however, do not come to school with the same literacy experiences.

The philosophy or mission statement of most schools acknowledges these individual differences and the fact that children do not all learn the same way, while the daily instructional program denies that same reality. Teachers are often told to teach whatever is "in." This happened with both the whole language movement in the 1980's, then again with phonics in the 1990's, and it happened at all grade levels. These programs worked for some children but not for all. Why? The reason is that different children learn differently! Children, even those in the same grade level, are at different stages of development. They are ready to learn different skills, and some of them are not ready for other skills without some prerequisites. Children, like adults, enjoy doing tasks in a way that is most natural or comfortable. How children learn and what they like to do varies from child to child just as it does from teacher to teacher. Children are not all stamped from the same cookie cutter. They do have real "individual differences!"

When students do not master a skill, or a set of skills, at a certain grade level in school, some teachers, administrators, and often legislators want these skills taught sooner and mastered quicker. Although this doesn't make sense to some, it does make sense to others. Over the last three decades, kindergarten has changed from a place of social development to a place where mastery of certain skills is expected. The solution for many educators is to "teach that skill in kindergarten so they will know it by the time they are in…." Other teachers, administrators, and child development specialists keep saying, "NO! These activities are not developmentally appropriate practices for the five-year-olds in kindergarten classes."

The solution for us is to teach children how to read and write, but to do it in a developmentally appropriate way. The past three decades have taught us much about how young children learn to read and write. We have used the research of others (Sulzby & Teale, 1991; Read, 1975; and Gentry, 1985) and even conducted some research of our own (Hall, 1997) to find out what works best and why. Using this research we know that you <u>can</u> teach kindergarten students about reading and writing without beginning a first and second grade program a year or two early. The idea is not to do it sooner, but to do it right. The Building Blocks framework was developed after the success of a primary grades framework, The Four-Blocks™ Literary Model, led some educators to believe that beginning this program sooner (in kindergarten) would lead to more success in reading. The originators quickly said, "NO," and the Building Blocks framework was born.

Why Not Four-Blocks in Kindergarten?

Over a decade ago, Patricia M. Cunningham and Dorothy P. Hall piloted a framework for multilevel, multimethod reading instruction in one first grade classroom with the help of an experienced first grade teacher, Margaret Defee (Cunningham, Hall, and Defee, 1991). The Four-Blocks™ Literacy Model represented four different ways to teach reading, and within each block, the teacher tried to be as multilevel as possible. Proven successful in one first grade class, the model quickly spread to second grade, as well as to other grade levels, teachers, schools, and states. Because children were actively involved in their learning, they were performing better on the standardized tests that many schools, school systems, or states require of their elementary students (Cunningham, Hall, and Defee, 1998; Cunningham, Hall, and Sigmon, 1999).

Using this framework, it was noted that some administrators had a renewed enthusiasm for school and many teachers had a renewed energy for teaching. Teachers who had taught for years saw a way to "do it all." New teachers found a framework to help them teach the many skills and strategies required at their grade level. Instead of assigning and correcting papers, teachers were engaged in activities with their students. One of the greatest problems with the spread of the Four-Blocks™ Literacy Model was the fact that many educators wanted to move this program into kindergarten (and upper grades) with very little in the way of modifications. Early childhood teachers were asking, "Is this developmentally appropriate for kindergarten students?" Some kindergarten students could do these tasks, but many kindergarten teachers knew that not all of their children had the literacy experiences that provided the necessary background their students needed to profit from some of these tasks.

We believe that a developmentally appropriate kindergarten is based on what children need to learn and what is known about how young children learn. In developmentally appropriate kindergartens, teachers accept all children regardless of their entering literacy levels, and take them forward on their lifelong literacy journeys.

> A developmentally appropriate kindergarten is like a good home, where children can learn through playing, cooking, watching, listening, acting, reading or pretend reading, and writing or pretend writing. It is a place where they can explore their environment, ask questions, and answer questions. It is a place where the teacher is like a parent—reading to the children and talking about the stories they read; writing for children and allowing them to write for different purposes; having time to explore their community on field trips; and talking about those experiences together. It is a place where children clean up after themselves, learn more about familiar and unfamiliar topics (usually called themes), and learn more about what interests them most—themselves. Most importantly, it is a place where children learn that reading provides both enjoyment and information, and they develop the desire to learn to read and write. (Hall and Cunningham, 1997)

Recognizing the developmental differences of kindergarten students, Cunningham and Hall were working with several successful kindergarten teachers, including Elaine Williams, to develop a kindergarten model (Hall & Cunningham, 1997; Cunningham & Hall, 1996). They wanted kindergarten students to see themselves as readers and writers regardless of their ability levels, and they observed that in certain kindergartens this was happening. They noticed that when the instructional program revolved around several concepts of emergent literacy development, then young students saw themselves as readers and writers. Thus, the cry for a developmentally appropriate kindergarten program became, "Building Blocks, not Four-Blocks!" and Elaine began her workshops with kindergarten teachers by saying, "I am here to tell you there is no such thing as Four-Blocks in kindergarten."

We call our kindergarten program Building Blocks, and we integrate Guided Reading, Self-Selected Reading, Writing, and Working with Words with the themes and units that are part of every kindergarten day. The blocks don't have a set time slot—and certainly don't each get 30-40 minutes every day. Four-Blocks is a framework for first, second, and many third grade classrooms; it is consistent with how primary teachers teach and how they schedule their days. Building Blocks is a kindergarten framework that is consistent with how kindergarten teachers teach and how they structure their days.

What Are The "Building Blocks"?

Recent findings from emergent literacy research have demonstrated that children who learn to read and write easily have a variety of experiences with reading and writing that enable them to profit from school literacy experiences (Cunningham & Allington, 1999). In kindergarten classrooms where teachers are using the Building Blocks framework, teachers provide a variety of reading and writing experiences from which all children develop these six critical understandings, which are the "building blocks" of their success:

- Children learn that reading provides both enjoyment and information, and they develop a desire to learn to read and write.

- Students also learn many new concepts and add words and meaning to their speaking vocabularies.

- Children learn prints concepts, including how to read from left to right, how to read a page from top to bottom, etc.

- Children develop phonemic awareness, including the concept of rhyme.

- Students learn to read and write some interesting-to-them words, such as "Pizza Hut," "cat," and "bear."

- Students learn some letter names and sounds usually connected to the interesting words they have learned.

Hall and Cunningham wrote a book about this program and named it *Month by Month Reading and Writing for Kindergarten* (Carson-Dellosa Publishing, 1997), but kindergarten teachers wanted more. While the format of this book is different from the *Month-By-Month* book, the philosophy, ideas, and some of the activities are the same. In addition, there are new examples and a more complete description of the kindergarten program in this book. We still do not try to do the whole day, but continue to focus on reading and writing—those early literacy activities that we now understand more clearly. There is still variation in the way these activities are used in different kindergarten classes by different teachers. It helps if teachers know when to do these activities and why they are doing them. Kindergarten is not a place to master skills. It is a place where caring teachers build a strong foundation for literacy learning.

Kindergarten is a place where a teacher needs to be every child's cheerleader and coach—helping these young students as they learn and cheering their progress, even if their steps are smaller than the teacher would have liked. The authors want kindergarten teachers to see that there are wonderful alternatives to worksheets, workbook pages, and memorization of letters, letter sounds, and words. These skill activities do not teach children, but rather, assess them. When doing these activities, some students are "bored" and other students "struggle." We hope to share with you our philosophy and our love for teaching as we describe some of our favorite activities so that everyone in the class can take an active role in learning. We want you to realize that all children are ready for kindergarten if you accept them where they are in their literacy journey and provide the experiences that they will need to move forward. Watching kindergartners grow is a most rewarding experience. It is rewarding for the kindergartners but even more rewarding for their teachers.

What Activities Build These Blocks?

Children who come to school reading, or ready to read, have had some reading and writing experiences that help them profit from school instruction. Teachers, like parents, can provide these experiences for all of their kindergarten students by following the activities within the Building Blocks framework:

1. Reading <u>to</u> children—both fiction and nonfiction

2. Reading <u>with</u> children—shared reading of predictable big books

3. Providing opportunities for children to read <u>by themselves</u>

4. Writing <u>for</u> children—morning messages at the start of the day and journal entries at the end of the day

5. Writing <u>with</u> children—shared writing of predictable charts

6. Providing opportunities for children to write <u>by themselves</u>

7. Developing phonemic awareness (the oral)

8. Working with letters and sounds (the written)

9. Learning some "interesting-to-them" words (names, environmental print, etc.)

Are All Kindergarten Students Ready for Building Blocks?

The answer is "yes," if your program includes multilevel activities, not just grade-level activities. Most children are five years old when they first enter school or kindergarten. Local school systems or state governments make this decision. Educators once thought that children would get "ready" for school in kindergarten and learn to read in first grade. Now, kindergarten is an essential and integral part of the total school program. Indeed, the foundation for all future school success is laid in kindergarten, hence the meaning behind the Robert Fulghum book *All I Really Needed to Know I Learned in Kindergarten*.

For many years kindergarten was a time to play and socialize. Next, came the skill and drill idea of the 1970's. Many educational programs were pushed down into kindergarten with few, if any, adaptations. The 1980's brought "emergent literacy" to the forefront of education, and we learned that teachers could help children learn how to read and write in a developmentally appropriate way—just like children who come to school reading. Workbooks, worksheets, and many "readiness" activities were put aside in favor of "real" reading and writing activities. These "real" activities were not only "developmentally appropriate" for children, but mirrored what happened in literate homes. The 1990's brought the cry for phonics, even at the kindergarten level. Proponents of phonics knew little about the need for phonemic awareness (the oral) before phonics (the written). Some phonics proponents even tried to say that their phonics workbooks and worksheets were helping to develop phonemic awareness.

Today, we know that young children learn about literacy from the day they are born, and maybe even before they are born. We can watch these young students develop into readers and writers as they participate in appropriate kindergarten literacy activities. Many activities appropriate for kindergartners are what we call "multilevel" activities. This means that these activities have something for everyone, regardless of their entering literacy levels. How is this possible? It is very easy to do, if you plan activities where you expect different outcomes from different students depending on their present abilities. Knowing how to make your activities multilevel frees kindergarten teachers (and parents) from worrying about the "top" or "bottom" kids in the class. We will explain how the activities in this book are multilevel after each one is introduced.

Children Change in Kindergarten; So Do Activities and Schedules!

What is a typical schedule for an all-day kindergarten? The answer to this question is not easy. State legislatures, school systems, and individual schools mandate the length of the school day and often the kindergarten curriculum. Building Blocks is a framework into which you put your curriculum. The amount of time kindergarten teachers have with their children, the ages of the children, and what previous experiences their children have had dictate to a large part what kindergarten teachers can and cannot do each day. One thing we know for sure is that if children are learning, the times and activities can and should change. On the following page, we offer a sample daily kindergarten schedule. This schedule will not reflect how these activities can change over the course of the year. The remaining chapters in the book will attempt to do this by giving sample lessons that require more and more from the students. We also offer a sample weekly schedule (pages 13-14) so teachers can see how the activities are not taught in isolation, but build upon one another.

These sample schedules are how one teacher organizes her day—this is not the only way to organize your daily activities. This particular teacher teaches in an all-day kindergarten, and this is reflected in her schedule. The possibilities for the schedule are virtually endless, depending on the time of year, the amount of time you have with the children, and the ability levels of the children in your class.

Daily Schedule for a Full-Day Kindergarten

8:30–8:45	Arrival: Greet students, early bird activities, table tasks
8:45–9:00	Announcements, Moment of Silence, etc.
9:00–9:30	Big Group, carpet chatter, discuss the day (themes, schedule, etc.)
	Getting to Know You activities (names)
	Calendar activities
	Weather Graph
	Calendar sentence strips (Today is. . .)
	Counting to 180 days of school
	Pledge of Allegiance
	Patriotic Songs
	Activity records/Tapes/CD
	Seasonal song or poem
	Phonemic Awareness activity
9:30–9:40	Morning Message
	Transitional activity (song/fingerplay)
9:40–10:10	Predictable Chart
	Transitional activity (movement/song)
10:10–10:40	Shared Reading/enrichment with big book
10:40–11:10	Specials (Art, Music, PE, Media Center, Computer, etc.)
11:10–11:45	Literacy activities (Journal Writing after 9 weeks)
11:45–12:15	Lunchtime
12:15–12:25	Hall/bathroom
12:25–12:50	Math
12:50–1:20	Outdoor PE or Recess
1:20–1:30	Cool Down – Snack
1:30–2:30	Centers (Teacher–directed/Student choice)
2:30–3:00	Quiet time/Story tapes or music
3:00–3:15	Prepare for Dismissal
	Get all things ready to leave, come to Big Group
	Discuss our day
	Sequence day's events
	Sing "Good-bye Song"
	Announcements

Weekly Schedule for a Full-Day Kindergarten—Early in the School Year

	8:30 - 9:00 Arrival	9:00 - 9:30 Big Group	9:30 - 9:45 Morning Message (Write 2 sentences)	9:45 - 10:10 Predictable chart	10:10 - 10:40 Shared Reading Big Book	10:40 - 11:10 Specials
Monday	(Wear red) • Color sheets & color word red • Announcements • Moment of Silence	• "Good Morning" Song • Getting to Know You • Calendar review • Pledge • Color songs, poems • Activity tape- movement • Read aloud <u>Brown Bear</u>	• Compare/contrast • Find: longest & shortest word • Print concepts • Track print • Circle words you can read	My Favorite Color is _____. Day 1 • Dictation	<u>Who Said Red</u> Before: Predictions During: Picture Walk After: Review predictions	Music
Tuesday	(Wear yellow) • Color sheets & color word yellow • Announcements • Moment of Silence	• "Good Morning" Song • Getting to Know You • Calendar review • Pledge • Color songs, poems • Activity tape- movement • Read aloud <u>Mr. Rabbit and the Lovely Present</u>	• Compare/contrast • Find: longest & shortest word • Print concepts • Track print • Circle words you can read	Day 2 • Complete dictation	<u>Who Said Red</u> Before: Read Book During: After: Discuss characters, setting, problem, ending Beach Ball	Media Center
Wednesday	(Wear green) • Color sheets & color word green • Announcements • Moment of Silence	• "Good Morning" Song • Getting to Know You • Calendar • Pledge • Color songs, poems • Activity tape- movement • Read aloud <u>Mary Wore Her Red Dress</u>	• Compare/contrast • Find: longest & shortest word • Print concepts • Track print • Circle words you can read	Day 3 • Read your sentences on the chart • Track print • Match words in your sentence	<u>Who Said Red</u> Before: Echo Reading During: After: Sequence- 1st, 2nd, 3rd, etc.	Art
Thursday	(Wear blue) • Color sheets & color word blue • Announcements • Moment of Silence	• "Good Morning" Song • Getting to Know You • Calendar • Pledge • Color songs, poems • Activity tape- movement • Read aloud <u>Blueberries for Sal</u>	• Compare/contrast • Find: longest & shortest word • Print concepts • Track print • Circle words you can read	Day 4 • Sentence builders	<u>Who Said Red</u> Before: Choral Reading During: Find Rhyming Words After: "Colors" song by Hap Palmer	Computer
Friday	(Wear purple) • Color sheets & color word purple • Announcements • Moment of Silence	• "Good Morning" Song • Getting to Know You • Calendar • Pledge • Color songs, poems • Activity tape- movement • Read aloud <u>Freight Train</u>	• Compare/contrast • Find: longest & shortest word • Print concepts • Track print • Circle words you can read	Day 5 • Book Making • Cut sentence strip (word by word). Put in order & illustrate	<u>Who Said Red</u> Before: Guess the Covered Word During: Act out book as it is read After: Eat colored popsicles	Teacher's Choice

Weekly Schedule for a Full-Day Kindergarten(continued)

11:10 – 11:40	11:40 – 12:25	12:25 – 12:50	12:50 – 1:20	1:20 – 1:30	1:30 – 2:30	2:30 – 3:15	
Literacy activities • Shape cut and paste red bird for book	Prepare for lunch Lunch Hall/ Bathroom	Math • One-to-one matching activities	Daily PE • Run the track	Cool Down • Snack- strawberries	Centers* Writing Center Complete color picture dictionaries • Write/trace color words and draw pictures	• Quiet Time Story /Classical tapes • End of day journal • Prepare to leave • Announcements • Sing "Good-bye" Song • Dismissal	Monday
Literacy activities • Shape cut and paste yellow duck for book	Prepare for lunch Lunch Hall/ Bathroom	Math • Tally marks Sets (1-5)	Daily PE • Run the track	Cool Down • Snack- pineapple	Centers* Art Center • Paint rainbows- red, yellow, pink, green, purple, orange, & blue	• Quiet Time Story /Classical tapes • End of day journal • Prepare to leave • Announcements • Sing "Good-bye" Song • Dismissal	Tuesday
Literacy activities • Shape cut and paste green frog for book	Prepare for lunch Lunch Hall/ Bathroom	Math • Tally Marks Sets (1-5)	Daily PE • Run the track	Cool Down • Snack- celery sticks	Centers* Science Center • Experiment with making colors	• Quiet Time Story /Classical tapes • End of day journal • Prepare to leave • Announcements • Sing "Good-bye" Song • Dismissal	Wednesday
Literacy activities • Shape cut and paste blue horse for book	Prepare for lunch Lunch Hall/ Bathroom	Math • What is your favorite color? Graph • Compare, contrast sets	Daily PE • Run the track	Cool Down • Snack- blueberries	Centers* Math Center • Graph colored candies. • Complete individual graphs of candies. •Compare & contrast	• Quiet Time Story /Classical tapes • End of day journal • Prepare to leave • Announcements • Sing "Good-bye" Song • Dismissal	Thursday
Literacy activities • Shape cut and paste purple cat for book	Prepare for lunch Lunch Hall/ Bathroom	Math Colorful Candy Graph (Individual graphs) • Graph your candy colors & compare	Daily PE • Run the track	Cool Down • Snack- grapes	Centers* Games • Play color teddy bear bingo game	• Quiet Time Story /Classical tapes • End of day journal • Prepare to leave • Announcements • Sing "Good-bye" Song • Dismissal	Friday

*After one daily teacher-guided center, students make choices.

Half-Day Kindergarten Schedule

For a half-day kindergarten, the schedule would have to change because you have less time! While you cannot do as much in a half-day kindergarten as you can with an all-day kindergarten, you can still integrate and accomplish the building blocks regardless of time.

8:30–8:45	Arrival: Greet students, early bird activities, table tasks
8:45–9:00	Announcements, Moment of Silence, etc.
9:00–9:30	Big Group, carpet chatter, discuss the day (themes, schedule, etc.)
	Getting to Know You activities (names)
	Calendar activities
	Weather Graph
	Calendar sentence strips (Today is. . .)
	Counting to 180 days of school
	Pledge of Allegiance
	Patriotic Songs
	Activity records/Tapes/CD
	Seasonal song or poem
	Phonemic Awareness activity
9:30–9:40	Morning Message
9:40–10:10	Specials (Art, Music, PE, Media Center, etc.) or Literacy Centers
	(Later in the year: journal writing/writing)
10:10–10:40	Snack/Break/Playtime
10:40–11:10	Predictable Chart /Shared Reading (Alternate Weeks)
11:10–12:00	Centers (including daily math activities)

Weekly Schedule for a Half-Day Kindergarten—Early in the School Year

	8:30 – 9:00 Arrival	9:00 – 9:30 Big Group	9:30 – 9:40 Morning Message (Write a one sentence message)	9:40 – 10:10 Specials	10:10 – 10:40 Snack/Playtime	10:40 – 11:10* Predictable chart	11:10 – 12:00 Centers** Math
Monday	• Schoolhouse color sheet • Announcements • Moment of silence	• "Good Morning" Song • Getting to Know you • Calendar • Pledge • Seasonal songs • Activity tape-movement	• Echo read • Count words in sentence • Find longest and shortest words	Music	Snack/Playtime	My Favorite Color Day 1 • Dictation	• One-to-one matching activities
Tuesday	• Bus color sheet • Announcements • Moment of silence	• "Good Morning" Song • Getting to Know you • Calendar • Pledge • Seasonal songs • Activity tape-movement	• Echo read • Count words in sentence • Find longest and shortest words	Media Center	Snack/Playtime	Day 2 • Complete dictation	• Tally marks Sets (1-5)
Wednesday	• Tracing shapes and coloring • Announcements • Moment of silence	• "Good Morning" Song • Getting to Know you • Calendar • Pledge • Seasonal songs • Activity tape-movement	• Echo read • Count words in sentence • Find longest and shortest words	Art	Snack/Playtime	Day 3 • Read sentence on the chart • Track print • Match word in your sentence	• Tally marks Sets (1-5)
Thursday	• Book Baskets • Announcements • Moment of silence	• "Good Morning" Song • Getting to Know you • Calendar • Pledge • Seasonal songs • Activity tape-movement	• Echo read • Count words in sentence • Find longest and shortest words	Computer	Snack/Playtime	Day 4 • Sentence builders	• What is your favorite color? Graph • Compare, contrast sets
Friday	• Market Baskets • Announcements • Moment of silence	• "Good Morning" Song • Getting to Know you • Calendar • Pledge • Seasonal songs • Activity tape-movement	• Echo read • Count words in sentence • Find longest and shortest words	Centers-Student's Choice	Snack/Playtime	Day 5 • Book Making • Cut sentence strip (word by word). Put in order & illustrate	• Sorting by shape and size

*Do Predictable Charts and Guided Reading on alternate weeks.   **After one daily math actvity, students make choices.

A Sample Day in a Building Blocks Classroom

Now you have some reference for why we use the Building Blocks framework in our kindergarten programs. You also have a time frame for using these activities in a kindergarten classroom. In the remaining chapters of this book, we will explain these activities in more detail. We will also show how these activities change throughout the year as the students learn more about reading and writing. Because all the pieces of the puzzle are important to achieving the greatest success within the framework, we want to take you on a visit to a Building Blocks classroom one fall day.

15 min.

Arrival

The children enter the classroom and prepare for the day. When they have their sweaters, jackets, show and tell items, and/or lunch boxes stowed, they go to a table and begin the table tasks. At some tables children assemble puzzles, while others string or sort beads. At other tables, children follow patterns with colored shapes or blocks. Sometimes, the children count dots and color in a picture. One table has a plastic crate filled with teacher-made little books. These books have pictures of characters from nursery rhymes and the rhymes that go with the pictures. It is easy to tell that these children have listened to and read these rhymes during the first few weeks of school and can all "read" them now. One child sitting at this table smiles as she pulls out a book and begins to read, "Jack and Jill went up the hill…." The teacher circulates and greets the children; helping those who need some help unpacking or getting focused on the table tasks.

Announcements/Attendance

Soon, the "breakfast bunch" returns from the cafeteria, and the principal is heard on the loud speaker with the morning's announcements. After greeting the students, he tells them the day of the week and the date. He also tells the students what they are serving for lunch in the cafeteria today. He mentions something special that will take place today ("The first graders will visit the fire station today."). Next, he reminds them that the PTA family fun night is this Friday evening, and tickets are still on sale. Finally, he asks all the children to sit quietly and observe the "moment of silence." The principal ends his announcements by saying, "Have a wonderful Wednesday!" As the principal talks, the teacher checks to see if all her children are in their places. She counts to 22 and looks to discover who is missing. She places an absent mark beside his name on the computer-generated attendance sheet.

"Big Group"

As soon as the principal finishes, the teacher is up and walking. It is time for "Big Group." The teacher stands at the front of the room, and the children recognize their cue and gather around her. She settles into a full-size rocking chair, while the children settle down on the carpet in front of her. They begin Big Group by singing the "Good Morning" song.

Next, some children raise their hands to share:

"My Daddy will take me to family fun night on Friday. My Mommy has to work."

"We went to eat pizza last night, and I saw John there with his family."

"I am going to my brother's soccer game after school today."

"My brother is reading a book about Harry Potter—I will read it when I get big!"

After a few minutes of quiet chatter ("Teacher says you have to use your quiet voices when you talk in class."), the teacher takes her turn and quietly announces that since they are learning about fall, she has a special book about fall to read to them today. She reminds them that Wednesday is the day they go to music with Mrs. Melody.

Next, she says, "Let's see who will be the leader and our special person today?" Without looking inside, the teacher draws a name out of a box which has the label "Getting to Know You" on it. Then, she announces that Corey will be the leader today. Corey quickly stands up, comes to the front of the group, and sits in a little rocking chair opposite the teacher. The teacher writes Corey's name on a piece of sentence strip with a big black marker . The teacher says each letter as she makes it, "C- o- r – e – y." Corey points to the letters in his name as he leads the familiar cheer.

"Gimme a C."	The children yell, "C."
"Gimme an O"	The children yell, "O."
"Gimme an R"	The children yell, "R."
"Gimme an E"	The children yell, "E."
"Gimme a Y"	The children yell, "Y."
"What have you got?"	The children yell, "Corey!"
"What have you got?"	The children yell, "Corey!"

The teacher then cuts the letters in Corey's name apart with four snips of her large scissors and places them back in the big blue pocket chart in random order. Corey picks the letters up one-by-one and puts them back in order, C-o-r-e-y, going from left to right. Next, Corey counts the letters in his name. He announces to the class that there are five letters in his name. Counting syllables in Corey's name is the next task. "Let's count the syllables in Corey's name," the teacher says. She claps twice as she says, "Cor-ey." Then, the teacher and the class clap together, once for each syllable.

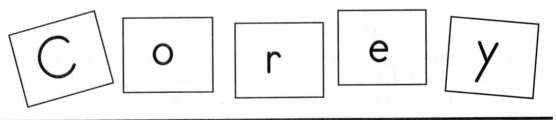

Then the teacher asks, "What do you notice about the letters and sounds in Corey's name?" Like the responses of most kindergarten students early in the school year, their answers are simple:

"I have five letters in my name like Corey," says Nancy.

"I have an *r* in my name too," says Brad.

"I have an *o* in my name," says John.

"I have a *C* at the beginning of my name like Corey," says Carly.

Emphasizing the beginning sound in Corey's name, the teachers asks the children if they know any words that have that same sound at the beginning. She makes a list on the chalkboard as the children tell her words they know that begin like Corey: cat, cake, cookies, car, cap, colors, cup, cone, Carolina, etc. Finally, Corey takes his place in front of the Big Group in a "special" chair for he is the "special" person all day long today!

The Big Group is sitting close by the calendar, which is the next task for the kindergarten class.

> "What month is it? Yes, it is October."

> "What day is it? That's right, it's Wednesday."

> "What is the date? It is the eighth. Can you count to eight? Let's count together: 1-2-3-4-5-6-7-8!"

> "What is the weather? That's right, it is sunny. Let's fill in our weather graph with a sunny day today. How many sunny days have we had so far in October?"

> "Let's fill in our sentence strips. Today is Wednesday. Yesterday was Tuesday. Tomorrow is Thursday."

> "How many days of school so far? Let's look above our calendar and count. Yes, thirty days of school. Let's all count to thirty: 1-2-3-4-5-6-7-8-9-10-11-12-13-14-15-16-17-18-19-20-21-22-23-24-25-26-27-28-29-30."

> "We have twenty straws in two bundles of ten, and now we have ten ones. Does anyone know what we need to do? Yes, we need to put a rubber band around these ten straws."

> "How many bundles do we have now? Right, we have 3 groups of ten."

> "How many straws are in these three groups? Yes, we have 30 straws for the 30 days we have been in school."

Next, the teacher hands the flag to Corey, the student of the day, who stands like a little soldier holding the flag. Led by the teacher, the students join in the "Pledge of Allegiance" and then sing "America" to the music on the tape recorder.

The next song on the tape recorder is one about colors by Hap Palmer. The teacher passes out different colored circles as the children follow the song ("Red stand up… blue stand up…yellow and green sit down…"). When they have completed the movements on the tape twice, the children once again are on the floor and looking at the big piece of chart paper the teacher has tacked to the board in front of them. It is a fall poem the teacher found in the Scholastic book *Interactive Charts*. The teacher reads each line to the class as she points at the words. The teacher talks about the color words in this poem. Next, she asks the children to find the rhyming words. The teacher points out how rhyming words sound alike, and she repeats these words orally as the children listen aurally to the rhymes.

Morning Message

The teacher stands to the left of the chart paper so that all the children in the class can see her write. She "thinks aloud" as she writes, "I always start each morning message with 'Dear Class.'" She writes D-e-a-r-space-C-l-a-s-s and spells it aloud as she writes. She continues, "Then I write my first sentence: Today is Wednesday. I use a capital letter at the beginning of the sentences because sentences begin with a capital letter. Today, T-o-d-a-y, is Wednesday, W-e-d-n-e-s-d-a-y. Wednesday needs a capital letter, too, because days of the week begin with capital letters. Next, I write my second sentence: It is a sunny day. I begin that sentence with a capital letter also (she says the letters of the words as she writes them), and I put a period at the end of the sentence. A period means that when I come to the end of a sentence I am supposed to stop. It is a sunny day—period. That means stop!"

"In my third sentence I will tell something we are going to do today. We go to music on Wednesday. I start my sentence with a capital letter and end the sentence with a period. My last sentence, the fourth sentence, is about Corey. Corey is our special student today." The teacher reminds the class that she always ends her morning message with the words "Love," and then her name, and she writes the words on the chart paper as she says them aloud.

> Dear Class,
>
> Today is Wednesday.
>
> It is a sunny day.
>
> We go to music today.
>
> Corey is our special student today.
>
> Love,
>
> Miss Williams

"Now, let's count the sentences. Yes, there are 4 sentences. Let's count the words in each sentence."

Today is Wednesday	3
It is a sunny day.	5
We go to music today.	5
Corey is our special student today.	6

She continues to ask questions about the morning message. "Which sentence has the most words? Which sentence has the least words? Which two sentences have the same number of words?" Next, she talks about letters, "Let's count the letters in each sentence."

Today is Wednesday	16
It is a sunny day.	13
We go to music today.	16
Corey is our special student today.	28

"Which sentence has the most letters? Which sentence has the least? Which two sentences have the same number of letters? Can anyone come up and find some words they can read in our message?"

Tracy says, "Is," and comes up and circles "is" three times with a red marker!

Mandy is called on next and she circles "today" in the message—three times!

"Can anyone come up and find two words that begin with the same letter?"

Steve comes up and underlines the W in "Wednesday" and "We".

"Can anyone come up and find a word that rhymes with play in our morning message?"

Janet finds the word "day" that rhymes with play.

"Good job!" says the teacher, as she gives the class a thumbs up sign. Next, the class stands and sings a song about the days of the week, and the children act out the words as they sing. This gives them some movement before the next quiet activity.

Predictable Chart
The teacher reminds her class that, "On Monday, I cut up some apples. The apples were red, yellow, and green, and each one of you got to taste a piece of each color of apple. On Tuesday, we made a graph in the pocket chart showing which color of apple was our favorite. Then, we wrote a chart about apples. We called it 'We Like Apples.' You told me which apples you liked, and I wrote a sentence for each of you. After each sentence, I wrote the name of the person who said it."

We Like Apples

I like <u>red</u> apples. (Corey)

I like <u>green</u> apples. (Mandy)

I like <u>yellow</u> apples. (Steve)

I like <u>red</u> apples (Tracy)

I like <u>red</u> apples. (Janet)

I like <u>yellow</u> apples. (Julie)

I like <u>green</u> apples. (Chris)

I like <u>yellow</u> apples. (Patty)

I like <u>red</u> apples. (José)

I like <u>red</u> apples. (Jim)

I like <u>green</u> apples. (Angelica)

I like <u>yellow</u> apples. (Jamarcio)

I like <u>red</u> apples. (Hannah)

I like <u>green</u> apples. (Michael)

I like <u>red</u> apples. (David)

I like <u>yellow</u> apples. (Julio)

I like <u>green</u> apples. (Ryan)

I like <u>red</u> apples. (Mathew)

I like <u>green</u> apples. (Suzanne)

"Today we are going to 'touch read' our sentences. This means we touch each word as we say it in our sentence. Corey, can you "touch read" the first one?" Corey goes up to the chart and touches each word as he reads, "I like red apples. Corey." "Good job!" says the teacher, "now it is Mandy's turn." After the children in the class have finished reading each sentence, the teacher congratulates them for their "good reading". She adds, "I didn't know everyone in this class could read!" From the smiles on their faces, the students are proud and can't wait to do "sentence builders" tomorrow and make another big book this week. They sing an apple jingle, do a finger play, and march around the room before gathering once again on the carpeted area.

30 min.

Shared Reading

It is now time for shared reading. The big book for this week is *Colors at the Zoo* by Phoebe Henderson (William H. Sadlier, 1998). Before reading the book again, the teacher shows the class the cover of the book and asks if they remember what this book is all about. Lots of hands go up and the child that is called upon says, "It is all about zoo animals and their colors." After a short discussion of what they remember, the teacher tells the class that today she will read the question on each page and see if they can read the answer. She begins reading. "What's blue at the zoo?" They join in, "A bird." The teacher and the children take turns reading the pages.

When they get to the end of the book they talk together about it. The teacher asks them, "What other animals might you see at the zoo? What colors are they? What was your favorite zoo animal? Why? What is your favorite color? Where else could you find animals?" The teacher lets the children read the book one more time. The last reading is done with the children's help. If they are wearing the same color as the page they are reading, they are to stand up as the page is read. When the teacher is finished reading, the children go back to their tables and are asked to draw their favorite animal at the zoo. The teacher reminds them that since this book is called *Colors at the Zoo,* they should be sure to choose the right color for their picture of a zoo animal. Soon it is time for their daily "Special." Today's Special is music with Mrs. Melody. The children line up at the door, and the teacher walks the class down the hall to the music room.

Music

Literacy Activities
When the children return to the room, the teacher has two pieces of folded paper for each student, stapled together like a book, on the tables. Each page has the sentences from the big book and a picture of an animal to color. The children read the pages with the teacher, touch reading each sentence in the "book." The children know that when they finish coloring the pictures and practice touch reading the sentences, they will be able to take this paper book home and read it to their family and friends.

Lunch (30 minutes); Hall/Bathroom (10 minutes)

Math

Outdoor Physical Education/Recess/Playtime

Cool Down/Story time/Listening
The teacher tells the children to get off their jackets and sweaters and tiptoe to the carpet. When she is at the front of the carpet, she looks at the class. They are all sitting like "pretzels" in front of her with their legs crossed. She picks up one of her big books, *Frederick* by Leo Lionni (Alfred A. Knopf, 1967). She reads the story of a little mouse who is a dreamer. All of the field mice, except Frederick, work to get ready for winter. The story ends in the cold of winter, with the field mice having used up their stored supplies, and Frederick telling the other mice to close their eyes as he describes all the warm colors he has stored in his mind. The teacher asks the children to close their eyes and see if they can see the colors as she rereads Frederick's poetic piece again.

60 min.

Center Time (Teacher Directed/Student Choice)

Art Center – Students paint an apple with their favorite color on large, manila paper.

Listening Center – Students listen to a taped story, *Johnny Appleseed*, and follow along with a book, turning the pages when they hear the "beep" on the tape.

Science Center – Students investigate/sort all kinds of nuts and seeds that appear in the fall.

Book Center – Students can choose what to read. This center has books about colors and fall, along with old favorites and new, easy predictable books. Class-made books are also stored here so the children can read and reread them.

Home Center – Students "make believe" that they are doing chores in the home (cooking, washing, caring for dolls, etc.).

Block Center – Students use blocks to make (create) something.

Math Center – Students count objects, including apples (if possible) and follow color patterns with beads and plastic geometric shapes. Other activity ideas include sequencing apple cut-outs from smallest to largest and weighing apples to see how many "teddy bear" counters it takes to balance the scale with one apple, two apples, three apples, etc.

30 min.

Quiet Time (Taped Story or Music)

15 min.

Prepare for Dismissal

Discuss the day.

Sequence the day's events (or write a journal entry).

Sing "Good-bye" song.

Listen to afternoon announcements.

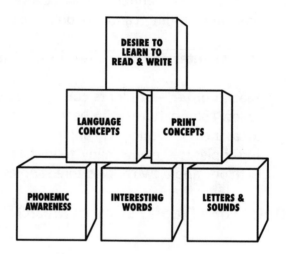

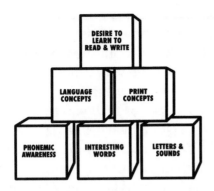

Chapter 2
Reading To Children

For many of us, being read to as a child was a familiar bedtime ritual. We cuddled up close to a parent and listened to a story every night. While a family member read the book, we had a chance to look at the pictures and discuss what was happening. We also had our first experience with print and the printed page. We soon learned that books were full of sentences ("What a long sentence that is!"), and sentences were made up of words ("Can you read all those words, Mommy?"). We also learned something about letters and sounds ("*Monday* and *morning* have the same sound at the beginning and begin with the same letter."). More importantly, we learned that books provided both enjoyment and information, and we developed the desire to read. In many homes today, television, video games, and computers have all but replaced this literacy event. Reading aloud to children every day in kindergarten ensures that all children have this valuable experience.

Benefits of Reading Aloud to Children

Research tell us that children who come to school ready to read have come from homes where they have been read to (Adams, 1991). *Becoming a Nation of Readers* asserts that reading aloud to children is the single most important activity for creating the motivation and background knowledge essential to success in reading (Anderson, Hiebert, Scott, and Wilkinson, 1985).

Children love books and stories. Kindergarten teachers have always recognized the importance of reading a variety of books to their students. It is hard to imagine any other activity that is so simple yet has so many benefits. In school, we read aloud to children because "reading aloud to children wakens their sleeping imaginations and improves their deteriorating language skills;" it also "improves children's attitudes toward books and reading." (Trelease, 1982).

Books and reading provide tranquility in the fast-paced world where we live. Bernice Cullinan says that books slow down the pace of life to a reasonable speed. Kindergarten is neither too early ("he can't sit still"), nor is it too late ("their parents haven't read to them") for any child. No activity does more than reading aloud to prepare a child for success in school (Cullinan, 1993).

Young children learn in many ways—from firsthand experiences and from vicarious experiences. Children come to school knowing about the world around them, but children who have not been read to often have very little knowledge about things they have not seen and places they have not visited. Books can take your students to far away places (*Africa, China, France*), or take you to places that are probably not so far away like a zoo, a farm, a city, a beach, or a garden. Books can help young children understand their problems (*Alexander and the Terrible, Horrible, No Good, Very Bad Day* or *Franklin Goes to School*), introduce them to a new friend (*Arthur* or *Clifford*), or let their imaginations run wild (*Where the Wild Things Are* and *Bat Jamboree*). Books can also help students learn math concepts (*One of Each, Fish Eyes*), learn about rhymes (*Mouse Mess* and *Miss Bindergarten Gets Ready for Kindergarten*), or learn the alphabet (*The Accidental Zucchini* or *Paddington's ABC*). Books can even introduce your students to new learning (*The Very Hungry Caterpillar* or *Pumpkin, Pumpkin*), or teach them about life long ago (*The First Thanksgiving* or *The Picture Book of Abraham Lincoln*).

When reading to a class, whether kindergarten or any grade level, teachers need to read both fiction (stories) and nonfiction (informational books).

Sense of a Story

When young children have been read fiction, they have a "sense of a story." They know the people in the story (the "characters"), and they can also tell you where it takes place (the "setting"). They know if a character had a problem (later called the "plot"), and how the problem was solved (the "solution"). The more young children are read to, the more they can tell you what happened at the beginning, middle, and end of a story. Young children who have been read to have a better chance of understanding both the vocabulary and the story elements that are introduced in the primary grades and talked about throughout their educational experience.

Information

Children need informational books to help build their background knowledge of people, places, and things. Children who live on a farm know a lot about farm life and have meaning for silo, tractor, plowing, fertilizing, etc. Children who have gone to the beach know about waves, seashells, and the tide. Other children who have gone on vacations to faraway places know more about the world than children who have not. How can young children learn more about strange places and unfamiliar things? Books! Books can take young children, just like they take teachers, to all the places they have not visited. We gain information as we read about those places. We gain information as we learn about animals like bats, panda bears, koala bears, fish, cats, wolves, sharks, etc. We also gain information as we read about things like cars, planes, boats, kites, trains, and games. We can learn about people who lived a long time ago such as George Washington, Abraham Lincoln, and Martin Luther King, Jr. We can learn about people who are living right now like Rosa Parks, Michael Jordan, and the president of the United States. Children who have been read to (and later in school, children who read a lot) have better vocabularies than children who have not had this opportunity. Children who have been read to are also able to profit from the instruction that takes place in school because they have more background knowledge about the things they will study in school.

Books can also take children and teachers on imaginary visits to places about which they can only dream. "Once upon a time" sometimes takes children to a time gone by (with dinosaurs, knights, dragons, princes, and princesses) or to a place that never was (*Alice in Wonderland*).

What Kinds of Books Do You Read to Children?

When asked to share their favorite read aloud book, most elementary teachers will share a favorite "story" or fiction. One national survey claimed that women bought 80% of the fiction sold in bookstores; it also reported that men bought 80% of the nonfiction sold in bookstores. Since most kindergarten teachers are women, it is not a surprise that the type of books that teachers enjoy reading to children is overwhelmingly fiction. Some children, and some teachers, like fiction, while some children, and some teachers, like nonfiction. When teachers read, they need to think about all the children in their class and read a variety of books!

Reading and "Blessing Books"

Linda Gambrell, a well-known reading researcher and writer who is now an administrator at Clemson University in South Carolina, has said several times during her talks that when a teacher reads a book to the class, she "blesses" the book. What books do children want to read or "pretend" read in kindergarten? They want to read the books their teacher has read to them! The books teachers read are thought of as "good" books! They contain "good" stories, rhymes, songs, or poems. Because someone has read this book to them, the children have knowledge of the characters, setting, and story. Using the pictures they can retell the story and enjoy the book again and again. After reading a book, the teacher may say, "If you picked up this book when you were visiting the "Book Center" how could you read it if you couldn't read the words?" Lead the children to say that they can tell the story now that they have heard it. You can then model this activity for your kindergarten class and "tell the story" as you look at the pictures, talk, and turn the pages (try this with *Three Little Pigs* or *Rainbow Fish*). When reading informational books or books with pictures and few words, they can read or "talk" the pictures (*Planes, Cars, Spiders,* or *Wonderful Worms*). Not only are teachers providing enjoyment and information, but they are also helping to show children that they can revisit these books by themselves even if they cannot read all the words.

Reading a Wide Range of Books, Levels, and Authors

When recommending books for kindergarten teachers to read aloud there are so many good books that it is impossible to do justice to the wonderful selection available today. Your local or school library is filled with many children's books, some of which have been favorites for years. You need to read these "old favorites" to your students. Many good books are recent additions to the library collection, and they also deserve your attention. In other words, teachers need to read both old favorites and the new "hits," some of which may have been missed. Some books have a "good" story for five-year-olds to listen to and other books are valued because of the pictures or the art that teachers show and share when they read. Children are interested in all kinds of information, and they want to know about the world around them. Children seem to get interested in anything teachers are interested in. Any book you enjoy is worth sharing, but the enthusiasm can be contagious when teachers share their favorite books!

Read-Aloud Books Recommended by Kindergarten Teachers
Books by Theme or Topic

ABC Books:

A You're Adorable by Buddy Kaye, Fred Wise, and Sidney Lippman (Candlewick Press, 1994).

ABC I Like Me! by Nancy Carlson (Viking Children's Books, 1997).

Accidental Zucchini: An Unexpected Alphabet by Max Grover (Harcourt Brace & Co., 1993).

Alphababies by Kim Golding (DK Publishing, Inc., 1998).

Arf! Beg! Catch! Dogs from A to Z by Henry Horenstein (Scholastic, Inc., 1999).

Color Books:

Color Dance by Ann Jonas (Greenwillow Books, 1989).

Brown Bear, Brown Bear, What Do You See? by Bill Martin, Jr. (Holt, Rinehart, Winston, 1967).

White Rabbit's Color Book by Alan Baker (Kingfisher Books, 1994).

I Went Walking by Susan Williams (Harcourt, 1989).

Purple, Green, and Yellow by Robert Munch (Annick Press, 1992).

Rhyming Books:

Miss Spider's Tea Party by David Kirk (Scholastic, Inc., 1994).

Zoo-Looking by Mem Fox (Mondo, 1996).

Golden Bear by Ruth Young (Houghton Mifflin Co., 1996).

To Market, To Market by Anne Miranda (Scholastic Inc., 1997).

Mouse Mess by Linnea Riley (Scholastic Inc., 1997).

Any book by Dr. Seuss

Books about Families:

Arthur's Family Vacation by Marc Brown (Little, Brown and Co., 1993).

The Quilt Story by Tony Johnson (Putnam Publishing, 1985).

What Will Mommy Do When I'm at School? by Delores Johnson (Aladdin Books, 1998).

The Doorbell Rang by Pat Hutchins (Scholastic, Inc., 1986).

Tucking Mommy In by Morang Loh (Orchard Books, 1991).

Our Granny by Margaret Wild (Houghton Mifflin Co., 1994).

The Relatives Came by Cynthia Rylant (Aladdin Books, 1985).

Books about School:
Miss Bindergarten Gets Ready for Kindergarten by Joseph Slate (Scholastic, Inc., 1996).

Franklin Goes to School by Paulette Bourgeois (Scholastic Trade, 1995).

Arthur's Teacher Trouble by Marc Brown (Little, Brown and Co., 1986).

Arthur Writes a Story by Marc Brown (Little, Brown and Co., 1996).

Miss Bindergarten's Hundredth Day of Kindergarten by Joseph Slate (Scholastic, Inc., 1999).

Books about Animals:
Arthur's Pet Business by Marc Brown (Little, Brown and Co., 1990).

Meow! retold by Katya Arnold (Holiday House, Inc., 1998).

My Friend the Gorilla by Atsuko Morozumi (Farrar, Straus, and Giroux, 1997).

Make Way for the Ducklings by Robert McCloskey (Viking Press, 1941).

Cats by Gail Gibbons (Holiday House, Inc., 1998).

Bats by Gail Gibbons (Holiday House, Inc., 1999).

Pigs by Gail Gibbons (Holiday House, Inc., 1999).

Rabbits, Rabbits, and More Rabbits! by Gail Gibbons (Holiday House, Inc., 2000).

Books about Vegetables:
Eating the Alphabet: Fruits and Vegetables from A to Z by Lois Ehlert (Harcourt Brace, 1989).

Pumpkin Pumpkin by Jeanne Titherington (William Morrow and Co., 1986).

It's Pumpkin Time by Zoe Hall (Scholastic, Inc., 1994).

Growing Vegetable Soup by Lois Ehlert (Harcourt Brace, 1987).

The Pumpkin Book by Gail Gibbons (Scholastic, Inc., 1999).

It's a Fruit, It's a Vegetable, It's a Pumpkin by Allan Fowler (Children's Press, 1995).

Books about Holidays:
Silver Packages: An Appalachian Christmas Story by Cynthia Rylant (Orchard Books, 1997).

The Year of the Perfect Christmas Tree by Gloria Houston (Econo-Clad Books, 1999).

Polar Express by Chris Van Allsburg (Houghton Mifflin Co., 1985).

Corduroy's Christmas by B. G. Hennessy (Scholastic, Inc., 1992).

Thank You, Santa by Margaret Will (Scholastic, Inc., 1991).

Santa's Favorite Story by Hisako Aoki and Ivan Gantschev (Scholastic, Inc., 1988).

Books about Famous People:
A Picture Book of George Washington by David Adler (Holiday House, Inc., 1989).

A Picture Book of Abraham Lincoln by David Adler (Holiday House, Inc., 1989).

A Picture Book of Martin Luther King by David Adler (Holiday House, Inc., 1989).

A Picture Book of Rosa Parks by David Adler (Holiday House, Inc., 1993).

I Have a Dream by Martin Luther King, Jr. (Scholastic, Inc., 1997).

Folk Tales/Fairy Tales/Retold Stories:
The Town Mouse and the Country Mouse by Helen Craig (Candlewick, 1992).

The Three Little Pigs by Eileen Grace (Troll Associates, 1981).

The Gingerbread Boy by Paul Galdone (Houghton Mifflin Co., 1983).

The Three Billy Goats Gruff by Allan Trusell-Cullen (Dominie Press, Inc., 1999).

The Three Little Pigs by Alan Trussell-Cullen (Dominie Press, Inc., 1999).

The Gingerbread Boy by Alan Trussell-Cullen (Dominie Press, Inc., 1999).

Cinderella by Alan Trussell-Cullen (Dominie Press, Inc., 1999).

The Frog Prince by Alan Trussell-Cullen (Dominie Press, Inc., 1999).

The Princess and the Pea by Alan Trussell-Cullen (Dominie Press, Inc., 1999).

Counting Books:
Five Little Monkeys Jumping on the Bed by Eileen Christelow (Houghton Mifflin Co., 1989).

This Old Man by Carol Jones (Houghton Mifflin Co., 1990).

Over in the Meadow by John Langstaff (Harcourt Brace, 1957).

My Little Sister Ate One Hare by Bill Grossman (Crown Publishers, 1996).

One Watermelon Seed by Celia Barker Lottridge (Oxford University Press, 1986).

Once There Were Twelve by Metro (Metropolitan Teaching and Learning Co., 1999).

The m&m's® Brand Counting Book by Barbara Barbieri McGrath (Charlesbridge, 1994).

The Crayon Counting Book by Pam Munoz and Jerry Pallotta (Cambridge, 1996).

Fish Eyes: A Book You Can Count On by Lois Ehlert (Harcourt Brace, 1996).

Rooster's Off to See the World by Eric Carle (Scholastic, Inc., 1997).

Number Concepts:
Just Graph It! by Sandi Hill (Creative Teaching Press, 1998).

Bear in a Square by Stella Blockstone (Scholastic, Inc., 1998).

One of Each by Mary Ann Hoberman (Scholastic, Inc., 1997).

Sea Squares by Joy N. Hulme (Hyperion Books, 1991).

Dealing with Addition by Lynette Long (Charlesbridge, 1998).

Fraction Fun by David Adler (Holiday House, Inc., 1996).

Eating Fractions by Bruce McMillan (Scholastic, Inc., 1991).

Books about Things That Happen to Five-Year-Olds:
Louie's Goose by H.M. Ehrlich (Houghton Mifflin Co., 2000).

Alicia Has a Bad Day by Lisa Jahn-Clough (Houghton Mifflin Co., 1994).

The Wimp by Kathy Caple (Houghton Mifflin Co., 2000).

When I Feel Angry by Cornelia Maude Spelman (Albert Whitman and Co., 2000).

Tom Goes to Kindergarten by Margaret Wild (Albert Whitman and Co., 1999).

Books about Things That Go (Transportation):
Boats by Byron Barton (HarperCollins, 1986).

Trucks by Byron Barton (HarperCollins, 1986).

Mike Mulligan and His Steam Shovel by Virginia Burton (HarperCollins, 1986).

Planes by Anne Rockwell (Dutton, 1985).

Trucks You Can Count On by Doug Magee (Putnam, 1985).

Truck Jam by Paul Strickland (Rugged Bears Publishing Co./Discovery Toys, 1999).

Lift-the-Flap Books:
A is for Animals: 26 Pop-Up Surprises by David Pelham (Simon & Schuster Children's, 1991).

The Jolly Postman by Janet and Allen Ahlberg (Little, Brown and Co., 1986).

Where's Spot? by Eric Hill (Putnam, 1980).

The Great Golden Easter Egg Hunt by Liza Baker (Scholastic, Inc., 2000).

Arthur's Neighborhood by Marc Brown (Random House, 1996).

What Can Rabbit Hear? by Lucy Cousins (Tambourine Books, 1991).

Good Night Books:
Good Night Moon by Margaret Wise Brown (Scholastic, Inc., 1989).

K Is for Kiss Goodnight: A Bedtime Alphabet by Jill Sardegna (Delacorte Press, 1994).

Bearsie Bear and the Surprise Sleepover Party by Bernard Waber (Houghton Mifflin Co., 1997).

Ira Sleeps Over by Bernard Waber (Houghton Mifflin Co., 1975).

Arthur's First Sleepover by Marc Brown (Little, Brown and Co., 1998).

Good Night! by Claire Masurel and Muriel Henry (Chronical Books, 1993).

Books with Poetry or Song:
I Know an Old Lady Who Swallowed a Fly, Vol. 1 by Nadine Bernard Westcott (Little, Brown and Co., 1980).

Old MacDonald Had a Farm by Prue Theobalds (Peter Bedrick, 1991).

Skip to My Lou by Nadine Bernard Westcott (Little, Brown and Co., 1989).

The Lap-Time Song and Play Book by Margot Tomes (Harcourt Brace, 1989).

This Is the Way by Anne Dalton (Scholastic, Inc., 1992).

Side By Side by Lee Bennett Hopkins (Simon & Schuster, 1988).

Multicultural Books:
Monkey-Monkey's Trick: Based on an African Folk Tale by Patricia McKissack (Random House, 1988).

Flossie and the Fox by Patricia C. McKissack (Dial Books, 1986).

Mufaro's Beautiful Daughters by John Steptoe (Lothorp Lee & Shepard, 1987).

Bringing the Rain to Kapiti Plain by Verna Aardema (Scholastic, Inc., 1981).

The Story of Ruby Bridges by Robert Coles (Scholastic, Inc., 1995).

Science Selections:
Stellaluna by Janell Cannon (Scholastic Inc., 1993).

Nests, Nests, Nests by Susan Canizares and Mary Reid (Scholastic Trade., 1998).

What Will the Weather Be Like Today? by Paul Rogers (Scholastic, Inc., 1989).

Frogs by Michael Tyler (Mondo, 1997).

Frogs by Kevin J. Holmes (Capstone Press, 1999).

Pigs by Gail Gibbons (Holiday House, Inc., 1999).

Spiders by Gail Gibbons (Holiday House, Inc., 1993).

Zipping, Zapping, Zooming Bats by Ann Earle (HarperCollins, 1995).

Wonderful Worms by Linda Glaser (The Millbrook Press, 1992).

Books About Favorite Characters
Arthur Books by Marc Brown:
Arthur Babysits by Marc Brown (Little, Brown and Co., 1992).

Arthur's Tooth by Marc Brown (Little, Brown and Co., 1985).

Arthur's Birthday by Marc Brown (Little, Brown, and Co., 1989).

Arthur's New Puppy by Marc Brown (Little, Brown, and Co., 1993).

Arthur's TV Troubles by Marc Brown (Little, Brown and Co., 1995).

Clifford Books

Clifford the Big Red Dog by Norman Bridwell (Scholastic, Inc., 1990).

Clifford's ABC by Norman Bridwell (Scholastic, Inc., 1986).

Clifford's Puppy Days by Norman Bridwell (Scholastic, Inc., 1990).

Clifford Gets a Job by Norman Bridwell (Scholastic, Inc., 1990).

Clifford's Good Deeds by Norman Bridwell (Scholastic, Inc., 1985).

Franklin Books

Franklin is Bossy by Paulette Bourgeois (Scholastic, Inc., 1994).

Franklin's New Friend by Paulette Bourgeois (Scholastic, Inc., 1997).

Franklin in the Dark by Paulette Bourgeois (Scholastic, Inc., 1991).

Franklin and the Thunderstorm by Paulette Bourgeois (Scholastic, Inc., 1998).

Franklin is Lost by Paulette Bourgeois (Scholastic, Inc., 1993).

Books by Favorite Authors

Tommie dePaola:

Strega Nona (Simon & Schuster Children's, 1979).

Big Anthony and the Magic Ring (Harcourt Brace & Co., 1979).

Strega Nona's Magic Lessons (Harcourt Brace & Co., 1984).

Jamie O'Rourke and the Big Potato: An Irish Folktale (Putnam, 1997).

The Cloud Book (Holiday House, Inc., 1984).

Eric Carle

The Very Hungry Caterpillar (Putnam, 1984).

The Grouchy Ladybug (HarperCollins Children's Books, 1996).

The Mixed-Up Chameleon (HarperCollins Children's Books, 1987).

Do You Want to Be My Friend? (HarperCollins Children's Books, 1971).

The Very Busy Spider (Philomel Books, 1985).

The Very Quiet Cricket (Putnam, 1997).

The Very Clumsy Click Beetle (Philomel Books, 1999).

Leo Lionni:

Swimmy (Alfred Knopf, 1991).

Frederick (Alfred Knopf, 1987).

A Busy Year (Alfred Knopf, 1992).

Alexander the Windup Mouse (Alfred Knopf, 1987).

The Biggest House in the World (Alfred Knopf, 1987).

William Steig:

Dr. DeSoto (Farrar, Straus, & Giroux, 1982).

Dr. DeSoto Goes to Africa (Harper Trophy, 1994).

Sylvester and the Magic Pebbles (Simon & Schuster Children's, 1988).

Brave Irene (Farrar, Straus, & Giroux, 1986).

Zeke Peppin (HarperCollins Juvenile Books, 1994).

Steven Kellogg

Johnny Appleseed (William Morrow & Co. Library, 1988).

The Island of the Skog (Dial Books for Young Readers, 1974).

Frogs Jump: A Counting Book illustrated by Steven Kellogg (Scholastic Trade, 1996).

The Mysterious Tadpole (Dial Books for Young Readers, 1993).

A Hunting We Will Go (Morrow Jr. Books, 1998).

Jan Brett:

The Mitten: A Ukranian Folktale (Putnam, 1989).

The Hat (Putnam, 1997).

The Gingerbread Baby (Putnam, 1999).

Trouble With Trolls (Putnam, 1992).

The First Dog (Harcourt Brace & Co., 1992).

Faith Ringgold

Tar Beach (Crown Publishing, 1992).

Dinner at Aunt Connie's House (Hyperion, 1996).

If a Bus Could Talk: The Story of Rosa Parks (Simon & Schuster, 1999).

Souvenirs

Souvenirs are concrete remembrances of a special trip, or a special experience. Do you collect souvenirs? Do you relive experiences as you come across your rocks, shells, menus, soaps, postcards, and matchbooks? Do you sometimes think about throwing away your souvenirs, but can't bear to part with them? Concrete, tangible objects are wonderful reminders of experiences. They trigger memories and help us relive the experience. Giving children a small souvenir after reading a book to them is one way to help them remember information they have learned and help them retell the story they have heard.

Some teachers call these souvenirs "story bits" because they are just a little "bit" of the story that help the children remember the story. We prefer to call them "souvenirs" because many of the texts we read are informational rather than stories. We don't want to confuse the children by using the term "story" for informational text. We like the idea of using souvenirs after a teacher-read aloud book, but we also feel they can be valuable prompts for retelling after Guided Reading.

Regardless of whether you call them "story bits" or "souvenirs," giving children something concrete is a wonderful strategy for helping them to remember the story or information, as well as helping them verbally practice the strategy of summarizing/concluding. If you keep your souvenirs simple, you will use them a lot more often. Remember the souvenirs are not there to represent the whole story or informational piece; they are only there to prompt the retelling of the story of information and to help the child remember. Some teachers include edible souvenirs. They pass out goldfish crackers after reading *Swimmy*, a cookie after reading *If You Give a Mouse a Cookie*, teddy bear graham crackers after reading *Golden Bear* (or any bear book), a piece of yarn after reading *The Mitten*, or a dog biscuit after reading a *Clifford* book. Other teachers want their children to make a collection of their souvenirs, so they give them cookies, fish, and bears cut out of paper, foil, or felt. Stickers make wonderful souvenirs and are better given as souvenirs than as rewards. There are also wonderful souvenirs to be found in different shaped pastas. A long piece of thick pasta will make a great wand or baton. Shell pasta will help children retell stories and books about the ocean.

Bean seeds would be wonderful souvenirs for *Jack and the Beanstalk*. Carrot seeds (*The Carrot Seed*), apple seeds (*Johnny Appleseed*), pumpkin seeds (*Pumpkin Pumpkin*), watermelon seeds (*One Watermelon Seed*), or any another important fruit or vegetable seeds, would make great souvenirs. Cotton balls work nicely for "bunny" stories.

Souvenirs is one of those ideas which most teachers have never considered. When teachers first hear about souvenirs, they think the items will be hard to find. But once teachers start looking, they see them in the rocks, seeds, crackers, and pieces of pasta that are part of everyday life. Better yet, the children begin to make connections between the real world and what they have been reading. After being given several souvenirs by his teacher, one enterprising boy arrived at school early one morning and proudly handed his teacher a bag of walnut shells. She asked expectantly, "What's this for?" The student explained, "It's the souvenir you can give everyone when we finish reading a *Franklin* book!"

How Reading to Children is Multilevel

Reading aloud to children is a simple, yet powerful activity. When the teacher reads aloud to her students, there can be something for everyone in the class, if the teacher reads a variety of titles, subjects, and levels of books. Some kindergarten children are just hearing these books for the first time. They need to have the books read aloud to them so that they can learn that books provide both enjoyment and information. Other children, who have heard the books before, are often recalling the events and remembering the details they have stored in their memories. They visualize what happens in their minds' eyes, which helps with comprehension. Other children know the books so well they can read or pretend read them when they are in centers or at home. Knowing the story or content of an informational book lowers the readability level of the book and makes it more accessible to all students.

When children are introduced to all kinds of books they may find a genre they enjoy and become real readers. By reading a simple chapter book (*Frog and Toad Are Friends* or one of the *Junie B. Jones* books) later in the year, teachers can model how good readers review what has happened in the story in their minds before they begin to read more. Listening to books as the teacher reads helps children with their listening skills. Kindergarten children are more apt to read a familiar book than an unknown book. Did you know that young children like to hear the same story over and over again until they make it their own?

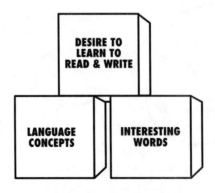

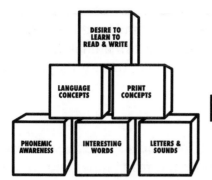

Chapter 3
Reading With Children

Shared Reading is one way to teach Guided Reading in the primary grades. Shared Reading is when teachers read <u>with</u> the children using predictable big books. In kindergarten classes doing Buildings Blocks, Shared Reading (including choral reading and echo reading) **is** the Guided Reading portion of the program. Shared reading provides children an opportunity to:

- experience print

- take notice of what print is doing

- experience words

- experience pictures

- experience and talk about the relationships between pictures and text

- experience reading with expression

Some kindergarten teachers have to use a basal reading program that has been adopted by their school or school system. The kindergarten portion of recently published basal reading texts includes a number of big books and sometimes multiple copies of little books that go with the big books. In other schools and school systems, teachers are free to choose their books and sometimes even the themes they want to teach. When teachers have big books, they can talk about both the story and the print on the page. Teachers can call attention to the pictures and discuss what is happening in the story, and then point to the print or text on each page.

Therefore, the question is not one of basal or big books, but how to teach reading effectively in kindergarten using big books. When we work with five-year-olds and big books, we let children share the reading by selecting books that fit into the unit or themes we are teaching. We also want to use predictable big books, so that after a few readings even the youngest of our students can join in and share the reading. In predictable books, the repeated patterns, refrains, pictures, and rhymes allow children to join in the reading of a book that has been read several times. The most important thing about Shared Reading is that even children in kindergarten with no literacy background will be able to "read" the book and develop the confidence that goes along with that accomplishment.

Many kindergarten teachers begin the year with familiar materials, like nursery rhymes, songs, and poems of the preschool days. These materials have the repeated patterns and rhyming words that make learning them so easy. They are also perfect for echo and choral reading.

Echo/Choral Reading

Echo reading is reading after the teacher. The teacher reads a sentence or page with not much text, and then the children "echo read," repeating what she read. Choral reading usually follows the echo reading of the same text. Choral reading works best for nursery rhymes, traditional rhymes and songs, poetry, refrains, and books with lots of conversation. The whole class can read the text together or the teacher can assign groups and parts to be "read" by different children. Kindergarten teachers often use old favorites, including nursery rhymes and finger plays early in the year, to do this. *Humpty Dumpty*, *Little Miss Muffet*, and *Twinkle, Twinkle, Little Star* are naturals for choral reading. Choral reading should be used throughout the year during the Shared Reading of big books because rereading provides children with the practice needed to build fluency and self-confidence.

We are going to illustrate a variety of choral reading activities with some nursery rhymes, traditional poems, chants, and songs. These titles are all in the public domain, which means that the author is unknown or that they are no longer copyrighted, and therefore, we can reproduce them in this book.

Nursery and Other Rhymes

Begin by reading the rhyme to the children. You may want to echo read it with them a time or two. Use a big book, if you have the rhyme in that format. If not, reproduce it on a chart. After reading it together, children enjoy pantomiming the rhyme while other children read it.

> *One, Two, Buckle My Shoe*
>
> One, two, buckle my shoe;
>
> Three, four, knock at the door;
>
> Five, six, pick up sticks;
>
> Seven, eight, lay them straight;
>
> Nine, ten, a good fat hen.

For *One, Two, Buckle My Shoe*, read the rhyme to the children the first time. The second time you read it, let the children be your echo and read after you as you cup your hand to your ear. The third time you read the rhyme, ask everyone to join in and read it with you. Once the children are familiar with the words, then you can begin to do some choral reading. To begin, you might have your children simply count off—1-2, 3-4, 5-6, 7-8, 9-10—and then get together by numbers. Everyone reads the title. Then, the children in the "1-2" group read the first line, those in the "3-4" group read the second line, those in the "5-6" group read the third line, those in the "7-8" group read the fourth line, and those in the "9-10" group read the fifth line. The children who are not reading can pantomime the rhyme. This way, every group has something to read or act out, making this activity quick, easy, fun, and fair!

Using the number of lines in the nursery rhyme to determine the number of groups is a good method for dividing the class, making sure to include a pantomiming group. For *Hickory, Dickory, Dock,* you would count off from one to six. The "one's" say the first line, the "two's" say the second line, the "three's" say the third line, the "four's" say the fourth line, the "five's" say the fifth line, and the sixth group does the actions. One group for each line plus one group of actors will also work nicely for *Jack and Jill, Hey Diddle Diddle, Twinkle, Twinkle, Little Star,* and *Humpty Dumpty.* You can read each rhyme five or six different times so the children will have a chance to do all the parts. Children's fluency is built as they read the lines of the poem several times. In addition, you can work on their sequencing skills by talking about what happened at the beginning, middle, and end of each rhyme. Sequencing and story mapping are skills that kindergarten teachers can work on if these skills are presented in developmentally appropriate ways—not with paper and pencil. These are also important skills that children are expected to know throughout their schooling.

Hey, Diddle, Diddle

Hey, diddle, diddle,

The cat and the fiddle,

The cow jumped over the moon.

The little dog laughed,

To see such sport,

And the dish ran away with the spoon.

Jack and Jill

Jack and Jill,

Went up the hill,

To fetch a pail of water.

Jack fell down,

And broke his crown,

And Jill came tumbling after.

Hickory, Dickory, Dock

Hickory, dickory, dock,

The mouse ran up the clock.

The clock struck one,

The mouse did run!

Hickory, dickory, dock.

Twinkle, Twinkle, Little Star	*Humpty Dumpty*
Twinkle, twinkle, little star,	Humpty Dumpty sat on a wall,
How I wonder what you are!	Humpty Dumpty had a great fall.
Up above the world so high,	All the king's horses and all the king's men,
Like a diamond in the sky	Couldn't put Humpty together again.

Later in the year, with longer rhymes and poems, you may want to assign groups to read verses rather than lines. Using the number of verses in the longer rhymes to determine the number of groups is a good method for dividing the class, making sure to include a pantomiming group if there are actions. We always begin by reading the poem to the children, and then having them read it with us several times. Next, we assign one group to read each verse and one group to do the pantomiming. Choral reading can be done using counting rhymes and rhyming songs, too.

For the traditional song, *Mary Wore Her Red Dress*, put the children in six groups, one group for each verse. If you know some actions for this rhyme, or can create some, be sure to assign a group of actors. The first time you read the rhyme, let the children look at the chart and listen as you read all six verses. For the second reading, let all the children read all the lines with you. This is an easy task because the children pick up the repetition and rhyme quite easily. For the third reading, call on Group #1 to be Mary and have that group read the four lines about Mary. Call on Group #2 to be Jim, and these children will read Jim's four lines. Group #3 is assigned to be Pat and reads her four lines. Group #4 is David and reads his four lines. Group #5 will read John's four lines. The sixth and final group is Amy, and they read her five lines. Depending on your class and the time of year, you may want to read this rhyme six times on six days in a row, or repeat it six times one day until all your students have gotten to be Mary, Jim, Pat, David, John, and Amy.

Mary Wore Her Red Dress

Mary wore her red dress,
red dress,
red dress.
Mary wore her red dress all day long.

Jim wore his blue coat,
blue coat,
blue coat.
Jim wore his blue coat all day long.

Pat wore her purple gloves,

purple gloves,

purple gloves.

Pat wore her purple gloves all day long.

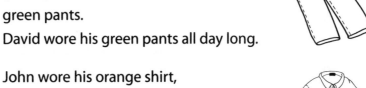

David wore his green pants,

green pants,

green pants.

David wore his green pants all day long.

John wore his orange shirt,

orange shirt,

orange shirt.

John wore his orange shirt all day long.

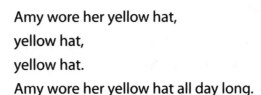

Amy wore her yellow hat,

yellow hat,

yellow hat.

Amy wore her yellow hat all day long.

The Wheels on the Bus, another traditional song, can be arranged and choreographed in a similar way. Make cards which say "wheels," "horn," "people," "driver," "children," "mothers," and "wipers." If you put pictures next to the words, it will help some students. Laminate the cards, put two holes at the top, and you have yarned necklaces to use year after year. On the first day, let all the children read all of the parts and do all of the actions with you. On the next day, divide the class into seven groups and assign each group to read a part. Each group will say their assigned lines and do the corresponding action. You will need to do this a few times, over several days, letting the children take turns with the parts so that everyone can do all the parts and the actions!

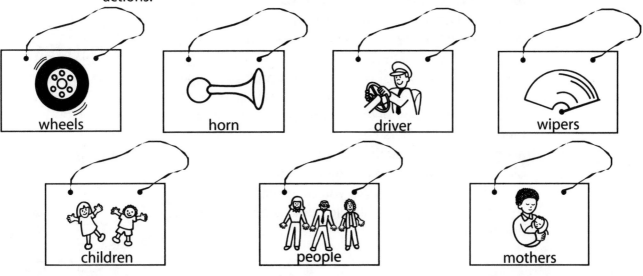

The wheels on the bus go round and round, round and round, round and round.

The wheels on the bus go round and round,

All through the town.

The horn on the bus goes beep, beep, beep, beep, beep, beep, beep, beep, beep.

The horn on the bus goes beep, beep, beep,

All through the town.

The people on the bus go up and down, up and down, up and down.

The people on the bus go up and down,

All through the town.

The driver on the bus says, "Please move back! Please move back! Please move back!"

The driver on the bus says, "Please move back!"

All through the town.

The children on the bus go, "Yak, yak, yak, yak, yak, yak, yak, yak, yak."

The children on the bus go, "Yak, yak, yak,"

All through the town.

The mothers on the bus go, "Shh, shh, shh, shh, shh, shh, shh, shh, shh."

The mothers on the bus go, "Shh, shh, shh,"

All through the town.

The wipers on the bus go swish, swish, swish, swish, swish, swish, swish, swish, swish.

The wipers on the bus go swish, swish, swish,

All through the town.

Shared Reading Using Predictable Big Books

In the Building Blocks framework Shared Reading is another way to teach Guided Reading whether you use a basal program or not. Most of the recently published basal programs have a combination of big books and multiple copies of little books. If teachers do not have a basal series that they must use, then they need big books in their classrooms. Kindergarten teachers need to have some big books that are predictable by picture or print, as well as some big books for "story book reading." If you are limited by what you have and what you can purchase, then remember that predictable big books are better for emergent readers.

Shared reading is usually done with a big book. The children gather around the teacher and the big book at a special spot in the room, sometimes in the front of the room, sometimes on one side of the room. Some teachers have big book stands to hold their books. Others put the big book on the ledge of the chalkboard or prop it against a table or a wall. The important thing is that all the children can see both the pictures and the print. The teacher guides the children through the reading of the book. She talks about the pictures and the print as she turns the pages. Thus, the teacher extends the lap experience and helps these young children learn how to use the pictures, print, and some key words in the book to learn more about reading.

What to Look for When Choosing a Big Book for Shared Reading:

1. The book must be very predictable, with repetitive sentences, pictures to support these sentence patterns, and not too much print.

2. The book should be enjoyable and appealing to most of the children, since the entire class will work with the same big book.

3. The book must be able to "take students someplace" conceptually. Most teachers spend a week or two with a book—reading, rereading, acting out the story, and building connections to themes or units to extend the children's knowledge.

(Hall and Cunningham, 1997)

With Shared Reading, as with any reading lesson, there is a before reading stage, a during reading stage, and an after reading stage.

Before Reading
Before reading, the teacher builds prior knowledge and gets the children ready to read by talking about experiences related to the book. If the teacher was reading *Pumpkin Pumpkin* by Jeanne Titherington, she would talk about pumpkins, and maybe even bring a pumpkin to school to show her class. She would talk about how to plant a seed and then watch it sprout. Next, the sprout grows into a green vine, then flowers appear, and finally a pumpkin grows. She might tell the class that there are more seeds inside the pumpkin. She could even cut the pumpkin, remove the seeds, and count them for a science/math lesson. The teacher talks about some of the "new" words in this book (seed, sprout, vine) that the children need to know to be able to understand the story. The teacher also allows time for the children in the class to share their own experiences with pumpkin patches and pumpkins.

During Reading
The "during reading" part of the lesson should involve the teacher reading the big book more than once. Shared, choral, or echo reading may be part of this phase. The first time the book is read to the class just for the enjoyment of listening to a good book. The second time the book is read by the teacher, she may want to have the children listen to the repeated pattern, "and the ____ grew into a ____." The teacher may also point to the words "and grew," which is repeated on pages later in the book. Pointing to the words as she reads them helps some children focus on both

the repetition of the sound and the repetition of the print. When the book is read for the third or fourth time, the children may join in the reading of this predictable text. They first begin to share the reading by being told to read the repeated patterns. Then, during subsequent readings, they will share in the reading.

After Reading

In the "after reading" part of the lesson, the teacher focuses on comprehension and understanding the story by leading a discussion and/or asking questions. Depending on which book was read, she may ask several questions about the "story," such as "Who?" "What?" "Where?" "When?" and "Why?" She may also ask, "How do you know that? What would you do? Was that right?"

The best way to help kindergarten students understand what the story is about is to "do the book" or "act it out." The teacher asks, "What characters do we need? Where was this story set? Who will talk first? What will he say?" In order to "do the book," students must understand the book. The teacher may use a "Beach Ball" with questions written on each colored stripe that are applicable for every story.

After reading, it is time to go from talking about the whole story to talking about the words in this story (long ones, short ones, rhyming ones, or repeating words). Finally, the teacher might talk about letters and/or letter sounds. She begins with the whole (the story or big book) and then goes to the parts (sentences then words then letters). At the sentence-level, she talks about the sentences. Then, at the word-level, she talks about words. Finally, she talks about the letters in some of the words and the sounds these letters make.

The Best Predictable Big Books

The best big books for emergent or early readers are those that are predictable by pictures or print. Two excellent examples of big books that are predictable by pictures are *Things I Like* by Anthony Browne (Houghton Mifflin Co., 1994) and *Moonbear's Books* by Frank Asch (Houghton Mifflin Co., 1996). In these books, children can "read the words" by looking at the pictures. The words are easily recognized because of the pictures that accompany them. If children are taught to look at the pictures and talk about what they see, they can often figure out the words ("riding a bike," "playing in the sandbox," etc.). When a kindergarten teacher stretches out the words she expects for each picture, some students can "cross check" and see if they are right by looking for the letters that they expect to appear in these words. For example, in the book *Things I Like*, when the little monkey lists all the activities he likes, the children can figure out the text for each page by looking at the picture and thinking about what the monkey is doing in the picture.

> "What does it say on this page? Yes, it says 'riding my bike' because you see the monkey on a little red bike, and you know he is riding his bike."

"Riding my bike" makes sense with the picture, sounds right, and makes sense with the sounds the students hear and the letters they expect to see. Predictable pictures allow young children to share the reading even before they are fluent at decoding many words. Thus, some books and stories are made easier for children because they are predictable by pictures.

Other books are predictable by print. In these books, words or a refrain are repeated over and over again in the text. As soon as the children can hear this pattern, they begin to chime in and share the reading of the story. Two examples of this are *Mrs. Wishy Washy* by Joy Crowley (Rigby Big Books, 1983) and *The Doorbell Rang* by Pat Hutchins (Scholastic Big Books, 1986). Once the children have heard the story, they can pick up the repeated pattern and join in or "share" the reading of the book. Students enjoy chiming in, "Wishy, Washy, Wishy, Washy," every time they see the refrain in the book. Big books not only allow children to hear the story, they allow children to see the print as well, just as they would if they were sitting on your lap. Once young children are familiar with the book, they begin to look at the print and notice many things about it. One thing they notice is that some words are big and have lots of letters and sounds (hippopotamus, helicopter, grandmother, etc.), while other words are little (dog, cat, no, pig, etc.) and do not have many letters. Sometimes they can sound out these little words, but the pictures and the beginning letters help more often with the big words. Always begin Shared Reading with the whole (the book or story), then go to the part (sentences and words), and then to the parts that make up the words (letters and sounds).

Sample Lessons Using Predictable Big Books

The following lessons will help you see how Shared Reading will look different depending on the students, stories, or content of the big books. You will also learn about the strategies that need to be taught to the students so that they can share the reading of the text more successfully. Here are some predictable big books you can use successfully in kindergarten for Shared Reading lessons.

Chicka Chicka Boom Boom

Chicka Chicka Boom Boom by Bill Martin, Jr. and John Archambault (Simon and Schuster Inc., 1989) is an example of a big book that is predictable by print in the first few pages and predictable by pictures if a child already knows the letter names! Young children love the lively, rhythmic flow of the text as they watch and listen to all the letters of the alphabet race each other up the coconut tree. "A told B, and B told C, 'I'll meet you at the top of the coconut tree.'" The large, colorful, lowercase letters of the alphabet are the "characters" in this big book. This book can also be found in a smaller size in both hardcover and paperback editions. Each page has bright colors for the letters and a simple picture of a coconut tree on it. The rhyming words, along with the rhythm that the teacher uses to read the book, keep children engaged throughout the early readings. Having heard the book just a few times, most kindergarten children are ready to join in. Some children may indeed be able to "read" this story because they have heard it many times and practiced it on their own. Other children may be able to recite the alphabet and recognize the letters by name after having spent some time with this book. Still other children may know the "story" after having a patient parent or caregiver read the book over and over until they memorized its rhythmic chant.

Children with limited literacy experiences before kindergarten can also grow from this or any other predictable big book. They will learn that books provide enjoyment and listening to them can be fun! They learn that you hold a book a certain way, you turn the pages in a certain way, and the pictures have something to do with those little squiggly marks on the pages. After reading *Chicka Chicka Boom Boom*, some children may learn that those marks are called letters. This is an example of a multilevel activity; there is something to be learned by everyone in the class regardless of their literacy level. As long as you do not have just one set of expectations for everyone, you can move the whole class forward in their literacy learning.

Before Reading: Talk About the Book

The teacher begins her lesson today with the big book *Chicka Chicka Boom Boom* on a big book easel. The easel is close by her "reading chair," where she does her "big group" or "whole class" activities. The teacher looks at the cover of the book and talks about what she sees, "Look at the green tree. Does anyone know what kind of tree this is? Look at these brown balls in the tree. Do you know what they are?" If anyone in the class had read the book, they would know that they are coconuts. Since no one knows what they are, the teacher talks about trees and the fact that some of them have fruit or nuts (like apple and oak trees), then she tells them about coconuts and coconut trees. (It would be wonderful to have a coconut for the class to open up, see the milk, and eat a piece of the coconut "meat" at science time later in the day.) The teacher talks about the authors (there are two for this book). Then, she talks about the illustrator, Lois Ehlert, who also wrote and illustrated another alphabet book, *Eating the Alphabet* (Voyager Books, 1989). The teacher also asks the children what they think this book will be about. Of course those that know the story already know it is about letters climbing up the tree until there are too many of them in the tree, and the letters "all fall down."

By asking the children what they think the book will be about, you will get your class wondering and asking themselves, "What will this book be about?" each time they pick up a book that is not familiar. If you model the process of looking inside the book for clues, then you will show all your students how to get more information about books. You will also help all children be more successful at the early stages of reading where pictures convey much of the information.

During Reading: Read the Book/Have Class Join in the Reading

The first and second reading of any book using a Shared Reading format should be strictly focused on the meaning and enjoyment of the book. Listening to *Chicka Chicka Boom Boom* is a special treat because of the rhyme and rhythm, so you may see heads and shoulders swaying to the beat! As you read it a second and third time, you may hear some children joining in on the refrain, "Chick Chicka Boom Boom! Will there be enough room?" The refrain is easy to pick up in the first part of this book. The remainder of the book does not have a predictable, repeated pattern or refrain, but is written in rhyme. This rhyme helps other children continue to be able to "share" the reading. As you look at each page, ask the children what they notice. Different children notice different things depending on their literacy level. You can tell by their responses whether they are focusing on the pictures, story, or print. Encourage the children to join in the reading of the early refrain and rhyming letters or words. Remember this is called Shared Reading!

After Reading: Act it Out

Young children are natural actors. They pretend they are all kinds of people and act out all kinds of situations. They do not need costumes or a stage, but are often thrilled with simple props. For *Chicka Chicka Boom Boom*, the teacher has chosen to draw large, colorful, lowercase letters of the alphabet on heavy drawing paper. She laminates the paper, punches two holes at the top, and ties yarn to them so that they can be worn like necklaces by the children. The children will become the letters and "act out" or "do the book." If the teacher does not have twenty-six children, then she needs to let a few children "be" more than one letter-character for this book. She is sure to act out the story more than once. The first time she reads the book, and the class mimics the parts. The next time, the children want to join in and share the reading. Reading and rereading gives young children a sense of "I can read" even if they are just joining in and sharing the reading. Memorizing a part in a play does not have the benefits that repeated reading of an easy book has on emergent readers. One of the first ways teachers can develop comprehension in young children is by "doing the book." This activity means that teachers have to talk about characters, setting, who talks first, how she says it, etc. All of this preparation focuses on what the story is all about, what happened, and why. These are all comprehension skills taught later in school, but understood so easily when children "act it out."

Make the Book Available

Make the book, or little versions of the book, available for children to read in the reading or book center. Once you have read a book several times with your children and acted it out, your students will all know how to read or pretend read it. You might want to read the book, or have the principal or a favorite adult read the book, and tape record it for a listening center. Young children delight in going to the listening center and listening to someone they know reading the book! Some children will just listen to the story, turning the pages at the appropriate time. Other children will be reading the words along with the voice on the tape. Still other children may be matching the voices with the print on each page and really reading!

Golden Bear

Golden Bear by Ruth Young (Houghton Mifflin, 1996) is about a little boy and his teddy bear. The little boy sees the bear everywhere—on the stair, in a chair, in the snow, in a tub ... even, "Dreaming dreamy dreams at night, Golden bear tucked in tight." The story can be part of a "nighttime" theme. It brings back fond memories for young children. They remember all the things they did with their teddy bears or tagalong toys, and they are reminded that they are never alone as long as they are sleeping with a "golden bear."

Before Reading: Take a Picture Walk and Make Connections

The teacher shows the children the cover of the big book. He points to the title and reads the name of the book, "Golden Bear." He points to the author's name and tells the class that Ruth Young is the name of the person who wrote the book. He calls the students' attention to the beautiful Afro-American boy and the great big golden-colored teddy bear on the cover. He also explains that Rachel Isadore drew the pictures (illustrations) in this book. The teacher builds prior knowledge for this story by talking about which children have teddy bears, what color their teddy bears are, how big their bears are, and what the children do with their bears. When young children talk about their experiences, they have an opportunity to make connections. It is easier for young children to learn and remember information if their brains can make some connections to their own experiences and knowledge. After several children have shared their experiences, the teacher tells the class that this story is about a little bear who seems to go everywhere with his friend.

The teacher then takes a "picture walk" through the book, talking about the bear and the boy. "What color is that? Let's see what they do together. Do they go up the stairs? That must be right because that word begins with 'st' just like 'stairs' begins with 'st.'" On the next page, the boy and his bear are rocking together in a rocking chair. The teacher points to the words "rocking chair" and says that those two words start with the right sounds. "We hear the 'r' sound at the beginning of 'rocking' and the 'ch' sound at the beginning of 'chair.'" He turns the page and talks about the violin under the boy's chin and the bear's chin, too! He talks about how to play the violin and make music. He goes on turning the pages and talking about the pictures: a rug, a bug, skating, some snow, a tulip, planting, some mudpies, a telephone, pirates, some clouds, dreams. There are so many wonderful pictures and words to discuss!

During Reading: Reading Aloud, Echo and Choral Reading, Shared Reading

The teacher reads the book *Golden Bear* to the class. He lets his kindergarten class listen to the story and enjoy it. He reads the book again and the children are asked to listen for all the things the little boy and the golden bear do together. The teacher may ask the children what they notice after each page. This question will lead children to a variety of answers rather than a one word or one sentence answer. The third time the teacher reads the book, the children are asked to listen for the rhyming words. The fourth time he reads the book, he asks his class to do an echo reading with him. He reads a page, cups his hand to his ear, and then the children read that same page as if they were his echo. Then, he reads the next page and repeats the procedure with the children becoming his echo. They continue this way for the remainder of the book. On other days he will echo read this story again, and then choral read the pages with the class. They may also do a Shared Reading where the teacher reads the story and those who know the pages "share" the reading with him.

After Reading: Discussion, Finding the Rhyming Words

After reading, the teacher discusses all the things the little boy and the bear did together. "Have any of you done these same things with your bear? Could these things really happen? What is your favorite page or picture?" (Our favorite is, "Cozy on a big green rug. Talking to a little bug.") The teacher leads the class to talk about the rhyming words they hear on each page. Since this is not the beginning of the year and his students can hear the rhyming words easily, the teacher has written these words on index cards and put the index cards in a pocket chart (or on the chalkboard) for the children to see. Next, he chooses a student to come up and underline the part of the rhyming pair that looks the same (b<u>ug</u>/r<u>ug</u>). He continues this activity with all the rhyming pairs except the first pair, where and bear. He adds, "This works most of the time, but not always." (If your students are having trouble distinguishing which words rhyme, do not go to the print [phonics] before they have mastered the oral [phonemic awareness]).

"Is this a real story or make-believe? It is probably a real story. A boy could really do these things and pretend that his bear is doing them with him. Do you take your teddy bear to bed with you? What do you take to bed? Why?" The questions for discussion are endless here. Choose a different topic to discuss, or a different activity to do each day as you "follow up" on your reading with an after reading activity. One idea is to integrate with your math lesson by drawing, then graphing, what the children sleep with.

The Very Hungry Caterpillar

This is an amazing story of a very hungry caterpillar. This little caterpillar has just popped out of his egg and is hungry, so he looks for something to eat. Every day he eats something different. The caterpillar is so hungry that he eats more and more each day. By the end of the week he has a stomachache and is big and fat. He builds a cocoon and after a few weeks, he turns into a beautiful butterfly. For some children there is a lot of new vocabulary in this book. Other children love to see the holes in the food (and the pages) as the caterpillar eats his way through one apple, two pears, three plums, etc. While reading this book, children again learn that books provide both enjoyment and information, in this case, the life cycle of a butterfly.

Before Reading: Build Background Knowledge (Picture Walk)

The Very Hungry Caterpillar has a captivating cover featuring a cute caterpillar crawling across the page. Scrunched in the corner, in all capital letters is the title, *The Very*

Hungry Caterpillar. The author/illustrator's name, Eric Carle, is smaller than the title. The teacher has the children look at the cover and enjoy this cute caterpillar. "Have any of you ever seen a caterpillar? Where? When? Did he look just like this?" The teacher could wait until spring to read this story. Then, she could bring in a live caterpillar so the class can compare it with the picture. The teacher also talks about the name of the book (title) and has a child come up and find it on the cover. She lets the child touch read the title, "The (1 sound, 1 touch) ver-y (2 sounds, 1 touch) hun-gry (2 sounds, 1 touch) cat-er-pil-lar (4 sounds, 1 touch)." This helps the children see that the bigger the word is, the more sounds you hear. Children who are ready to learn to read have already made this connection during the lap experience. Talking about this helps the children who have not had this experience take notice of the print. It also reaffirms those students that have noticed big word and little words before.

Next, she takes a picture walk through the book. The first page of the text has a dark picture. "What time of day is it here? Look at the moon and the leaf on this tree. What do you suppose that is on the leaf? An egg? On the next page is a caterpillar. What happened to that egg? Do you think the words here will tell us?" The teacher turns the page and pauses for a moment for the "oohs" and "aahs" of the kindergarten children as they see the different size pages and all the different fruits to eat. "Each piece of fruit has a hole in it! Let's look at all these pages. What is on this page?" She lets the children share their knowledge and make connections because most children are familiar with these fruits. For children who have not had experiences with all kinds of fruits and for children who are just learning to speak English, this will build vocabulary. The teacher has brought in one of each fruit, unlike the book that has one apple, then two pears, then three plums, and so on. The teacher chooses one or two fruits and lets the class "cross check" with her. "We know from our alphabet books that apple begins with an 'a.' Can you find the word 'apple' on this page? Pear begins with a 'p.' Can you find the word 'pear' on this page?" Looking at the next page, the children can see lots of different fruits with holes in them. The teacher asks and gets them to think, "Why do you think there is a hole in the fruit on each page? Do you think the words on these pages will tell us? Maybe, we will have to read and see."

The teacher continues her picture walk and turns the page again, "Here is a 'nice green leaf' with holes in it and that hungry caterpillar again. Do you think he ate holes in the leaf, too?" Turning the page once more, the teacher points to a big, fat caterpillar, and she talks about how this caterpillar is different from the cute little one we saw before. "What has happened to him?" (She notices how the children stretch out their tummies as they talk about the caterpillar eating so much!) She calls attention to the cocoon and then the two-page spread of a beautiful butterfly by saying, "What do you think this story is about?" After this picture walk the children are ready to read. During the teacher's picture walk, the children made some predictions using the pictures and text. Now they want to hear the story and see if their predictions are right!

During Reading: Shared Reading

The first reading of this book is just for enjoyment. The teacher reads the book aloud, pausing occasionally for the children to take in all the pictures on each page before turning to the next page. She emphasizes the pattern when she reads about the days of the week and what the caterpillar eats on each day. "On Monday, he ate through.... On Tuesday, he ate through.... On Wednesday, he ate through...and so on." Some children already want to join in the reading. The pictures from the picture walk are helping them with their reading of the words (or memorization). The teacher reminds the class that they must first listen to the book, "We listen to the book the first time so that students who have not heard the story can do just that. I will let you help me read it the next time." Once the teacher finishes, the children beg to hear the story again. The second time the teacher reads the big book, she tells the class that she will read all the words except for when she pauses. At this time, they can read or say the words. On the first page, she points to the words as she reads them, pausing for the words egg and leaf, "In the light of the moon a little ...egg... lay on a ...leaf." The teacher and the children continue to share the reading of the book.

After Reading: Discuss the Book, Sequencing, Sentence Builders

There is a lot to discuss after reading this book, such as caterpillars, cocoons, butterflies, fruit, food, cause and effect, life cycles, etc. All of these discussions can be done in a developmentally appropriate way. The teacher began by guiding students through a picture walk using the big book. Next, the teacher guided them through the reading and Shared Reading of the text. Now, the teacher guides them through a discussion of the book. The teacher and the children discuss what the caterpillar ate each day of the week. The teacher might want to write the days of the week on sentence strips and sequence them in the pocket chart when she discusses what happened each day. If the students are sitting near the large class calendar, she might want to have a child point to the days of the week at the top as they discuss what happened each day. Next, the teacher and the class discuss all the different food the caterpillar ate on Saturday, "Why did the caterpillar eat through the nice, green leaf on the following Sunday?" Finally, the teacher and class discuss how this caterpillar became a butterfly. The children may want to pretend that they are caterpillars, cocoons, and then butterflies. Young children love to pretend!

Another "after reading" activity is to choose a sentence from the book and do "Sentence Builders." The teacher chooses the sentence, "On Monday, he ate through one apple." She writes this sentence on a piece of lined sentence strip with a thick black marker. She cuts the words apart with a pair of scissors—-snip after "on," snip after "Monday," snip after "he," snip after "ate," etc. The teacher tells the class she is going to pass out the words and see if they can build the sentence using their words. She asks the children who are holding the word cards to come to the front of the group and "build their sentence." One child ("On") notices that he is first, so he quickly goes to the left side of the other words. "Monday" notices that her word is next and that she is second, so she takes her place. The little boy with "he" wanders over to the book, turns to the page with the sentence they are building and counts, "One, two, three" and gets in his place. The first child in line tells "ate" to get in the next place in the sentence as he points to the correct spot. "Through" is the biggest word and the child holding that card is proud to take the next place. The boy with the word "apple" knows he is last because he has a period after his word. He directs the little girl with the word "one" to her spot to the left of him. The sentence is now complete. The teacher says to the class, "Let's read the words and see if they built the sentence just like it was in the book. (She points to each word) On…Monday… he…ate…through…one…apple. Good job! Good job, sentence builders." This activity may be repeated with other sentences, but do not do too many. The teacher reminds her students that they will get to do this again when they ask for more. Children love to "be the words" and become "sentence builders!" (There is a starter chart for this activity in CD-2505 Building Blocks™ "Plus" for Kindergarten.)

It's a Perfect Day
In the book *It's a Perfect Day* by Abigail Pizer (Scott Foresman, 1990), it is a perfect day; a perfect day to crow thinks the rooster; a perfect day to take a nap thinks the cat; a perfect day to wallow in the mud thinks the pig, etc. All the animals in the barnyard have perfectly different ideas about what to do on this perfect day. Kindergarten children will find this a perfect excuse to make animal noises (cock-a-doodle-doo, buzz, purr, moo, quack, oink, squeak, honk, woof, etc.) as they join in and share the reading of this repetitive, cumulative story!

Before Reading: Picture Walk, Make Connections
Before reading this big book, the teacher has her kindergarten students look at the cover and talk about the animals on it. There is a familiar dog and cat. For children who have been read to, or who live on a farm, the cow, pig, horse, rooster, duck, and goose may be familiar, too. The teacher points out that the name of the book is written across the top of the cover. Next, she has the children look at the picture on the cover, "Where do you think this story takes place? What makes you think that?" The author's name is at the bottom of the cover. The teacher tells the class, "Abigail Pizer wrote this book," as she points to the name on the cover.

Now the teacher is ready to turn the pages and take a picture walk through the book. The pictures will help the children know which animals are on this farm. The animals are the "characters" in this book. On the first page, the animals are asleep and the children have to look closely to find them. They will delight in finding the animals, coming up to the big book, and pointing to each animal as they say its name. After the teacher and the children discuss the first picture, she turns to the next page and asks, "Does anyone know the name of this animal? What does this animal say?" The teacher and the class turn the pages and discuss the different animals, what the animals are doing, and what the animals are saying. By looking on the left hand pages, the teacher and the class can also see that the number of animals is cumulative and growing until all ten are on the last two pages.

During Reading: Shared Reading
This is a perfectly wonderful book to read to young children, but be prepared for your class to want to chime in and make the noises. Many preschool children have learned to make all the animal sounds. Young children love to show off, and this

book allows them do just that. They really want to share the reading of these repetitive animal noises! Be sure to remind them that you want them to listen the first time you read the story, and be prepared for some of them to be too excited to just listen. The second reading is a good time for you to do most of the reading and let the children "help" by making the animal noises. This is also an excellent book to let children read a "part" as you, the narrator or story reader, read everything else. You will have to do this more than once as everyone will want to be an animal, and some parts are more valued or bigger than others! Young children cannot get too many readings of this big book.

After Reading: Discussion, "Doing the Book"

This is an easy story to discuss. The pictures show just what each animal wants to do that day. There is a lot of vocabulary building for some children. For other children, it is a joy to share their knowledge with the class. Regardless of ability level, this story is fun for five-year-olds! It is hard to read this story to children without seeing that most of them would love to "act it out" or "do the book."

Since ten animals are the characters in *It's a Perfect Day*, you could choose ten different children to be the ten animals and wear yarned necklaces, or you could have two children for each animal. If you don't have enough children, the "little ones," the mouse and the bee, could be represented by only one child. If you have more than twenty children you can have three children represent some of the animals. Whatever you do, let everyone have a chance to be an animal, show off, and "do the book."

One day, instead of reading the book, you could put ten sentence strips in a pocket chart, sequence the sentences, and then reread the sentences in the chart, with each child reading the sentences of their respective animal parts. This is also a wonderful book to record the reading of on a tape or CD as you "do the book" with the class. For weeks to come, children will want to listen to themselves if you make their recordings available in the listening center.

Gingerbread Boy

Before Reading: Build prior knowledge of gingerbread boys, baking, etc.

During Reading: Shared Reading; repetition of pattern, "run, run, as fast as you can"

After Reading: Open-ended questions about the book, make puppets, act it out

On the following page is an outline of the plan for what the teacher will do. The next decision is to plan the before, during, and after reading activities for each day, since the teacher and the class will use this book for a week or two. Here are some other things to think about if you want to enrich your students' learning while reading this book.

1. You can combine this with a theme/unit about the five senses (see, taste, smell, hear, touch).

2. Make and bake a big gingerbread boy in the cafeteria. When you go to get him, he is gone! Search the school looking for the gingerbread boy.

3. Read several different versions of this book (there are many on the market) and discuss what is the same about each story and what is different. Graph the similarities and differences, then let children choose their favorite version.

4. Paint gingerbread men with brown paint on construction paper, or sew and stuff gingerbread men, cutting them out of brown bulletin board paper and decorating them with paint or yarn.

The goal of the Shared Reading experience is for the child to eventually take the shared book and be able to successfully pretend read it.

What to Do When Working on One Book for a Whole Week

1. **Before Reading: Introduction**
   - Read the title of the book, author, title page, and dedication.
   - Predictions: Look at the cover of the book.

        What is the story about?

        Is the story real or fiction?

   What else can you learn from the pictures?

   - Picture Walk: Model and guide good picture walk skills.
   - Use a pointer (wand) when focusing children on pictures, text, or tracking print. This way, you won't block pictures or text.

2. **During Reading:**
   - First Reading: Read through the book non-stop, allowing children to experience the book without interference.
   - Second Reading: Students might start to chime in naturally while you read.

3. **After Reading:**

   At the end of the second or third reading, start working on comprehension:
   - Who? What? Where? When?
   - Name the main characters.
   - Is there a problem present?
   - Build the next level of thinking—What would you do? What could happen next? Why do you think that happened?
   - Tossing a Beach Ball with general comprehension questions written on its stripes is a fun way to work on comprehension.

4. **Future Reads: Third, Fourth, Fifth, etc.**

   Start paying attention to specifics:
   - Find rhyming words in the text.
   - "Be the Words": Children spell words with letter vests.
   - Echo reading: This is essential to help understand the flow, rhythm, and emphasis of the big book.
   - Choral read: Mix up ways to choral read.

        Groups can rotate pages as they read.

        One group can read all but the last word, then the other group reads the last word.

   - Practice the Cloze technique or Guess the Covered Word by using "stick-on" notes.
   - "Do the book" and act it out.

5. **Place the Book in the Reading Center**

Souvenirs

In Chapter 2, we talked about giving the children souvenirs of books we have read aloud to them. A souvenir is a reminder of a pleasant experience. Children like to collect things, and if you provide souvenirs regularly, as they are reading they will begin to wonder, "What will she give us to remember this book?" This is the kind of pleasant and anticipatory association you want to build for reading. Souvenirs are "little things" which mean a lot to children. Souvenirs bring back memories of a book you have read or places you have been. When we use souvenirs in connection with something read during the Shared/Guided Reading block, we spend a few minutes with children "practicing" what they will tell their family and friends when they take their souvenirs home. Some examples of souvenirs are making caterpillars out of egg cartons when you finish *The Very Hungry Caterpillar*, giving students a colorful, cut-out alphabet letter after reading *Chicka Chicka Boom Boom*, sharing a teddy bear graham cracker after *Golden Bear*, or giving them animal crackers after *Zoo-Looking*. After reading a book with the class and receiving a souvenir from their teacher, the children can practice their retelling of the story with a partner or share it with the whole group. Now they are ready to go home and show off in more ways than one.

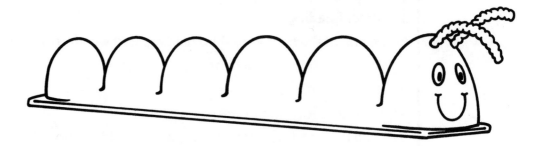

"Storybook Reading" Using Big Books

When a big book is not predictable by pictures or print, or there is too much text on a page to do a shared reading of the big book, then the big book can be used for "storybook reading." Storybook reading is when a big book, or any other size book, is read aloud to the class solely for the enjoyment of the story. When there is a large amount of text, the teacher is not able to call attention to the repetitive patterns or the print. Because the print is too small for most children to notice, you have to simply read the book and talk about the story. You can still do before, during, and after reading activities. For example, before you read, take a picture walk and talk about the pictures but don't call attention to the print because it is too small for all to see. You can still read the story and discuss it after asking what the children noticed on each page; however, noticing the print is difficult, and with some books impossible, unless the children are sitting very close to the teacher. The children can still "do the book" and "act it out;" they just have to paraphrase their parts rather than reading their parts as they can do with the simpler text.

Darrell Morris commented on storybook reading at his session during a recent National Reading Conference (Morris, 1999). He said that "storybook reading" was a common practice for most kindergarten teachers. We feel that young children enjoy good stories in any size book, but there needs to be some teaching about print in kindergarten (more on this in chapters 8, 9, and 10) so predictable big books must be a integral part of the kindergarten reading program.

How Reading With Children Is Multilevel

Children who come to kindergarten already beginning to read move further along in their reading as they learn more about words. Having an opportunity to observe both the pictures and the print, they begin to notice similarities and differences in words and learn to read even more words. Children who come to kindergarten with little or no print experience learn what reading is and develop their concepts of print. Other children learn a few words and begin to notice how words are the same and different. They gain confidence with the knowledge that they are learning to read. Most importantly, kindergarten children develop the desire to learn to read and write. They are also learning letter names, language and print concepts, phonemic awareness (rhyme), and maybe some interesting-to-them words as they share the reading of big books and learn to read in a way that is developmentally appropriate for five-year-olds.

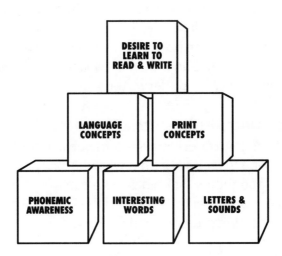

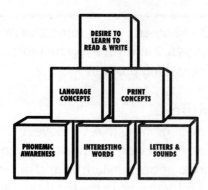

Chapter 4
Children Reading by Themselves

Young children need time to read or pretend read by themselves in order to develop an "I can do it attitude." Kindergarten teachers need to provide opportunities for their students to read books of their choice. Independent reading is an important part of a balanced reading program, even in kindergarten. Kindergarten classrooms are famous for their centers—the home center, building center, art center, writing center, Reading Center, science center, etc. It is in these centers that children explore and discover their environment individually or in small groups. This chapter on children reading by themselves is divided into two parts. The first part focuses on the reading centers, an important part of the kindergarten program all year long. The second part focuses on children reading by themselves— "Self-Selected Reading" at school or "take-home reading." In kindergarten, when we begin Self-Selected Reading, it is a brief period (5 –15 minutes), with each child reading a book of his choice. It does not begin on day one; it begins later in the school year after all the children have had exposure to a number of books and have strategies for "reading" these books by themselves. The number of books and the reading levels of the books and materials available in the classroom can make this a very multilevel activity for kindergarten students.

Teaching Students the Three Ways to "Read"

A commonly observed phenomenon in homes where preschoolers have books and someone to read to them is what we call "pretend reading." Young children want to do all the things that big people can do. They pretend they are a mommy, daddy, teacher, or nurse. They pretend they can drive, mow the yard, cook, and even read! They do this pretend reading by themselves, to a younger child, or to a stuffed animal.

We teach our kindergarten students that there are three types of reading:

- You can read by reading all the words (teachers and some children can do this).

- You can "pretend read" by telling the story (anyone can do this).

- You can "picture read" by looking at the pictures in a book and talking about the things you see (anyone can do this).

After reading a book to the class, help your children decide how they might read the book if they picked it up in the Reading Center (and later in the year during Self-Selected Reading) and could not read all the words.

> "This is an alphabet book. You can see one picture on each page and a word that goes with the picture. If you look at the pictures, you can probably read the words."

> "*Little Red Hen* is a book you can probably "pretend" read because you know the story. Let's practice how you might pretend read it and retell this story."

> "This is a book about zoo animals. If you can't read the words, you know the names of zoo animals, so you could look at each picture and talk about the animals you see."

Once children know that there are three ways to read, there is never a reason for a child to say, "I can't read yet!"

Reading in Centers (All Year)

Learning Centers are an important part of a developmental kindergarten program. It is in these centers that children explore and discover their environment individually or in small groups. There are two things to remember when setting up the Reading Center. The first is that the children should have a comfortable place to read alone or with a friend. The second thing to remember is to have lots of good books and other reading materials from which they can choose.

       63   *The Teacher's Guide to Building Blocks*

The Reading Center (or Book Center) should be a pleasant, cozy place. Some teachers use leftover furniture that has been donated to the classroom. Other teachers are fortunate enough to have their schools buy child-size chairs and sofas, or build a reading loft. If you work for a school or school system that provides furniture and reading materials, you are fortunate. Most teachers want to add accessories—a Humpty Dumpty lamp, a little Pooh rug, a large picnic basket or colorful barrel in which to store books, a small beach chair, etc. Often these items are from a flea market, bought on sale, or hand-me-downs from home.

The books that the teacher has read to the class during teacher read-aloud are always popular in the Reading Center. "Old Favorites," stories they have heard many times or books that were read to them many times before they entered kindergarten, should also be included. Informational books and magazines need to have their special place in any Reading Center. Books about the different themes studied in kindergarten need to be available, as long as the theme is the topic of class discussions. As the school year progresses, class books and student-authored books can be added to the Reading Center.

Every kindergarten classroom is filled with reading materials. Teachers often add to this from a variety of sources including home, the school library, the public library, the bookstore, friends, fellow teachers, or any other available source. Some materials that are popular in Reading Centers are children's magazines and store catalogues. These can be low-cost or no-cost if they are brought from the teacher's home or donated by the students' families. Many book companies and bookstores have books for teachers to purchase at reduced rates, and all the popular trade books are now in paperback. You will also save a lot of money if you teach your students to take care of things that have value, like books! If you are buying books to display on a shelf, then don't spend your money. Books are for reading!

Lately, predictable texts have become favorites of teachers, students, and parents because the children can read them easily once they notice the predictable pattern in the text and know how to use the pictures to help with the words. Sunshine and Wright Group were two of the first companies to publish these easy predictable paper books. Now many companies, including basal companies, have added collections of small predictable books. Among these collections are *AlphaKids Alphabet Books* by Sundance Publishing. These books are sold in single copy sets of 26, one for each letter. The Alphabet books start with real kids' names, shows words that begin with the target letter, and progress to complete sentences. Also available from the same company are *Little Blue Readers*. These *Little Blue Readers* are non-fiction books with predictable text and visual clues that support emergent readers. They feature forty high-interest titles with stunning real-life photographs for clear word-picture connections. The *Little Blue Readers* can be purchased in single copy sets of 40 books, one of each title. Celebration Press also has a number of big book versions of the popular titles of their little books and classroom library sets. Predictable books with repeated patterns are an easy way for some children to learn to read. Do not forget all the children in your class, and provide as many different types of books in the Reading Center as possible.

When reading in centers, some kindergarten students will look at the pictures and learn from these books. Other students will just talk away as they "pretend" read and learn from these books. The students that can "really read" will have an opportunity to do so and become even more fluent at reading. The more a child reads a book, the more practice she has with reading and the better she will get at reading. When parents and peers brag on these little readers, they become more intrinsically motivated to read. Real readers do not read for pizza, points, or stickers—they read for the pleasure and joy of reading! We believe that praise is the best reward you can give these young readers if you want them to turn into lifelong readers. The Reading Center is a special place where you can sit a child on your lap and share some "quality" time with a book; there is no finer gift or reward!

While a quiet room is valued by many teachers, it is important to note that many emergent readers—kindergartners included—have trouble reading or pretend reading silently. Kindergarten children like reading a book together, talking about the book, and even acting out the story. Other kindergarten students will read by themselves but this reading is done aloud. Mommy reads aloud to them, daddy reads aloud to them, and the teacher reads aloud to them; so many young children think that reading should be aloud. When some children are learning to read, they need to hear themselves read to make sure they are saying the correct words. If a book is difficult to read, adults (like young children) want to say the words aloud. Somehow it helps to hear yourself!

Reading the Room Center (All Year)

Another center that is becoming popular is the "Read the Room" Center. Here children use a "magic wand" or special pointer to go around pointing and "reading" the words in the room. They read color words, number words, the months and days on the calendar, the weather words, the words in the Writing Center, and words on charts and books. Reading the room helps children learn to read, and it also helps them when they write. Reading the room provides a valuable source of correctly spelled words for young children to use when they are writing. When kindergarten children get used to reading the room, they know where to look in the room for certain words they need when writing. By writing these words correctly again and again, many young children not only learn to read the words, they often learn how to spell (write) these words. Some children like this strategy more than others. This is because some children like to write words correctly and not use their invented or "developmental" (sound) spelling.

Reading the room is often done with a partner. The two children take turns, with the "pointer" partner going around the room pointing at words in centers, on charts, or on signs, while the other child reads the words. The pointing partner praises the reading child and then leads her to other sets of words in the room.

Self-Selected Reading (Later in the Year)

When all of your children have had the experience of reading in centers and they know how to read the pictures or the book, you are ready to have the whole class read for a short period of time. We call this our Self-Selected Reading time because the children are allowed to choose or "self-select" the books they want to read, just as they are allowed to do in the center. As you begin this activity, you may want to teach "whisper reading" to your students by modeling it.

Self-Selected Reading is part of a balanced reading program in elementary school. It is one of the blocks in the Four-Blocks™ Literacy Model in primary grades. However, reading for a sustained period of time is very hard for young children until they are used to this behavior at home or at school. When your class is ready, usually in the spring of the year, some of your books will "leave" the center and become part of the book baskets. Teachers put the books in baskets, dishpans, or plastic crates. These book baskets are placed at tables of 4-6 children. The purpose for the baskets is so the children can have their books close by and not have to wander across the room to get another one when they are finished with their first book. We have noticed that the children who wander the most are the children who need to read the most.

Teachers try to fill each of the four or five book baskets with a variety of books. The book baskets contain books the teacher has read aloud to her students, books used for Shared Reading, favorite books, books by favorite authors, and books on the themes the class is studying. The teacher strives to provide the kinds of books children in kindergarten can read, or books they enjoy pretend reading. Teachers make sure that some of these books are good books for practicing skills the children have learned during Shared Reading. Teachers also make sure there is "something for everyone" in the book basket at each table or area. As we have said before, most kindergarten children cannot read quietly, but they can lower their voices. Set the clock for five minutes during the first week, or until they start to ask for more time to read. Increase the time a minute or two each week until almost all of your students are occupied with a book for the entire time period and are asking for more time to read when the timer goes off. When the class has reached 15 minutes of reading time, continue with this amount of time for the remainder of the school year. What is important is that children have a place to read, and they can self-select their books from a variety of materials that they can read and want to read. The teacher's role in Self-Selected Reading is to roam around the classroom, drop an ear and listen, and "ooh" and "ah" at the students' attempts at reading. This is also a time when the teacher can "coach" a child or two that might need some extra help when reading.

Take-Home Reading (Later in the Year)

Until children can read independently, the expectation is that parents will read to and with their children nightly. We know this is not possible in all of the children's homes, but we can hope! Once you get kids hooked on reading by reading aloud to them at home and in school, they are more apt to have the desire to learn to read.

Reading a book repeatedly leads children to "pretend" read that book, and later to really read the book. Later in the kindergarten school year, a take-home reading program is useful. A take-home reading program provides books to parents and their children who do not have books in their homes.

Kindergarten teachers send home "take-home readers" in brown clasp envelopes or large resealable plastic bags. Simple directions are given to the parents to follow:

Let your child read to you. If your child has difficulty reading the book, you read a sentence and let your child read it after you. Encourage your child to touch the words as you read the book together. It is okay if your child wants to read the book more than once, and remember . . . praise, praise, praise!

The reward children get for reading should simply be the enjoyment of the book itself. Parents and teachers should not stress the number of books read, or the difficulty or length of the books. Every child should be praised for what they can do. When self-selecting books, young children often choose to read favorites books and stories over and over. Let them! The more they read, the better they will become at reading. Take-home reading promotes the enjoyment of reading and, when done correctly, can become a lifetime activity of relaxation and enjoyment.

How Reading by Children Is Multilevel

When kindergarten students read by themselves in centers, at Self-Selected Reading time, or at home, some of them will just look at the pictures and learn from the books that way. These students are the ones who need time to handle books. They discover that books are held a certain way and pages are turned a certain way. They also learn that you can tell what the books are about by looking at the pictures. If they have learned some familiar words, they will look for these words in the text. They cannot read yet, but they know enough about books to mimic the activity. Other students will "pretend" read and learn from the books. These children often know the story, use the picture clues as prompts, and think they know what to say on each page. The kindergarten children that can "really read" will have an opportunity to do so and will become even more fluent at reading. When kindergarten children choose what to read at school and at home, they are on their way to becoming lifelong readers. When children read by themselves, it can be a multilevel activity in kindergarten, provided that the teacher has a variety in the number, level, and kinds of books available for children, and they can read or pretend read the books of their choice.

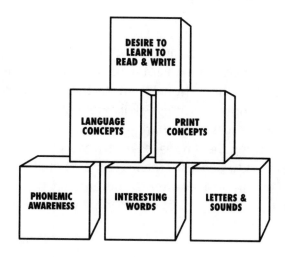

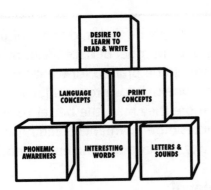

Chapter 5
Writing for Children

When teachers write for children they provide a model for writing. Children need to know how people think as they write and what they do when they write. Early in the school year, when the teacher writes the morning message, a sign, a schedule, directions, or a journal entry at the end of the day, she has an opportunity to model how she writes for the class. As the children watch and listen, they begin to understand what they are to do when they are asked to write. Later in the school year, the teacher and the students become interactive as they write the morning message together (Chapter 6). This chapter will help you understand the importance of writing for children. It will help you see how your class will benefit not only from watching you write daily, but also from hearing you think aloud as you write. There are sample lessons from three activities that teachers use to write for children—the morning message, signs and directions, and journal entries.

Young children learn many skills, such as swimming, dancing, and soccer, by first watching a family member, friend, teacher, or coach do the activity. Then, when they are ready, children will try it themselves! This can also happen when a teacher writes a morning message. It is one of the most powerful ways to help children understand what writing is and how people think as they write. For children further along in their literacy learning, watching the teacher write a daily morning message can move them quickly towards independence in writing.

Watching children year after year, we have noticed that more and more kindergarten children are coming to school either reading or knowing a little about reading. However, children do not usually come to kindergarten writing. Most children from literate homes—homes where they see someone reading and writing—know something about these skills. However, some children do not have homes where books, pencils, pens, markers, crayons, or paper are available. They have not seen an adult using these tools to write grocery lists, letters, notes, or messages. Some youngsters hold a pencil for the first time when they enter school or during the kindergarten screening a few months before they begin school. For these children, it is essential that teachers show them what writing is before asking them to do this task!

Morning Message

Many things happen each day in school, and kindergarten students often look forward to what is going to take place. They may think to themselves and sometimes ask aloud, "Is it art day or music day?" "Will we read a familiar book or one I have never heard before?" "Who will be the 'special person' today?" It is a good idea in kindergarten for the teacher to write a morning message every day. This morning message is written on a large piece of lined chart paper with a thick, black or some other dark-colored marker. Many teachers do this activity as part of the opening or right after the class meeting. Other teachers write their morning message when they call the big group together for Shared Reading. The first morning messages are simple, using just a sentence or two like this:

Dear Class,
Today is Tuesday.
We will go to
music today.
Love,
Miss Williams

Each day as the teacher writes and talks about what she is writing, she lets her students know what she is writing and why she is writing it. For the first few messages, the teacher will be doing all the work and the children will be listening and learning what to do and why.

"I am going to write a morning message. I will say the words as I write.

"**Dear**, capital D-e-a-r, **Class,** capital C-l-a-s-s. This is a **comma** (pointing to the comma), and it means to pause."

"The first sentence I am going to write is, **Today is Tuesday. Today**, Capital T-o-d-a-y, **is**, i-s, **Tuesday**, capital T-u-e-s-d-a-y." The teacher writes a period and points to the period while saying, "This is a period. You put a period at the end of a sentence."

"Now I am going to write the second sentence, **'We will go to music today.'** **We**, capital W–e, **will**, w-i-l-l, **go**, g-o, **to**, t-o, **music**, m-u-s-i-c, **today**, t-o-d-a-y. I put a period at the end of this sentence," she says as she points to the period.

"At the end of my letter, I write the closing. I like to say, **'I love you.'** **I**, capital I, **love**, l-o-v-e, **you**, y-o-u, **comma**." The teacher points to the comma she has just written and says, "Pause."

"I end the message with my name, so that you will know I wrote you this message. **Miss**, capital M–i-s-s, **Williams**, capital W-i-l-l-l-i-a-m-s."

"That is my morning message to you. It tells you what day it is and what we will do today."

"Let's look at the first sentence," she says as she points to the first sentence. "How many words are in the first sentence?"

"Let's count the words in the first sentence and see." The teacher encourages the children to join her in counting the words, "One, two, three." Next, the teacher uses a colored marker to write the numeral three after the first sentence.

She points at the second sentence. "Let's count the words in the second sentence. One, two, three, four, five." The teacher uses the same colored marker to write the numeral five after the second sentence.

"Which sentence has more words?" The teacher calls on a child who raises her hand. "Right, the second sentence has more words. It has five words."

"Let's count the letters in the first sentence, 1-2-3-4-5-6-7-8-9-10-11-12-13-14. There are fourteen letters in the first sentence."

"Let's count the letters in the second sentence, 1-2-3-4-5-6-7-8-9-10-11-12-13-14-15-16. There are sixteen letters in the second sentence."

"Which sentence has more letters?" The teacher calls on a child to answer her question. "You're right! The second sentence has more words and more letters!"

Skills Taught When Writing Morning Messages

When writing the morning message during the first months of school, the teacher should concentrate on saying the words and writing the letters as she says them. Kindergarten students should not be expected to learn to spell these words. However, many will learn the letter names and be able to recognize letters because they hear the teacher say the letters as she writes them day after day. When writing morning messages early in the school year, the teacher should concentrate on:

- what you say, you can write

- where to start writing and which way the writing goes (left to right)

- where to begin the next sentence or line (top to bottom)

- saying the words, then saying each letter, one at a time, as it is written

- using capital letters

- using punctuation

- counting sentences

- counting words in sentences

- counting letters in sentences

- finding out which of the sentences has more words/ letters

- clapping the sounds you hear in words, like today (to-day)

- talking about how you start and end a message

- talking about the things that happen each day

- talking about special events that happen to students in the class

(See the Morning Message chart in CD-2505 Building Blocks "Plus" for Kindergarten package to begin.)

After several weeks, the teacher begins to ask her kindergarten students:

- Can someone show me where I start my morning message?

- What sound do you hear at the beginning of that word?

- What letter do I write at the beginning of that word?

- Will I begin that word with a capital letter?

- What do I put at the end of that sentence?

- What do I put at the end of that question?

- How do I show that we are excited about going?

- How do I end my sentence?

- Can anyone help me spell the word 'love'?

- Does anyone know what letter to begin 'Miss' with? 'Johnson'?

- Can you find a word you know and circle it?

- Can you find a word that begins like _____?

- Can you find a word that rhymes with _____?

An example of a morning message written during the second quarter, after the students have been in school awhile, might look like this:

Dear Class,

Today we will learn about the Pilgrims.

Do you know about the first Thanksgiving?

We will learn about the first Thanksgiving.

Love,

Miss Williams

By this time, the teacher will write the morning message, but she might not spell every word she writes. She might write, "**Dear Class,**" and then ask, "Who can read what I just wrote?" After 40-50 days, most children know what the teacher writes to begin the morning message. The smiles on the children's faces will show you how proud they are of this new accomplishment.

The teacher continues to write her message each morning, saying the words as she writes. On some days the teacher writes the opening and closing lines without saying them aloud and asks if anyone in the class can read them. She knows that most of the children can. She chooses a student to do this, and then praises the student's "good reading." The teacher also tries to use more than one kind of sentence so the children can see periods, question marks, and exclamation marks being used. After the writing and reading of the morning message, the teacher may ask her kindergarten students:

- To count sentences and words. Which is the longest? Shortest?

- What do you notice about the morning message?

- Who can find a word they know in the morning message?

- Who can find a word in the morning message that rhymes with ___?

- Who can tell me how this word starts (what letter or letters)?

- 'Dear Class.' What kind of a letter do I start 'Dear' with? (capitalization)

- What do I put at the end of this sentence? (punctuation)

Young children often enjoy the time spent reading and writing the morning message. Often, we see children who want to write their own morning message at home and at school. Sometimes these children bring in their morning message to read to the class. One day, a student walked into his kindergarten classroom and proudly announced to the teacher and class, "I have the morning message for today!" Below is what he wrote at home, probably with some help spelling the words. You can see that this young student not only knew what writing was, but also how you write and why he was writing the message (to tell about a special day).

Dear Class,

Today we will go to the fair.

I love you.

Miss Williams

Jake takes the morning message one step further when he comes in with a morning message the next day, written from the class to the teacher! This is Jake's morning message:

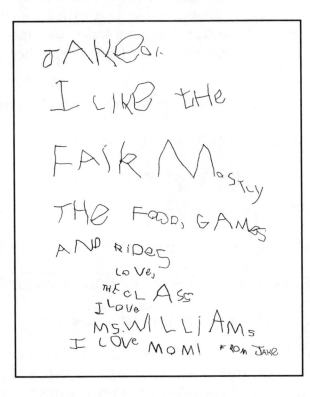

I like the fair. Mostly the food, games, and rides.

Love,

The Class

I love Ms. Williams.

I love Mom!

From Jake

Journal Entry at the End of the Day

A wonderful way to begin journal writing is to end each day by talking about what your kindergarten class did that day, and then to write about it while the students watch you. Many teachers end each day with a class meeting to discuss what happened in school that day. This will help your youngsters remember what they did when their parents or guardians ask that famous question, "What did you do in school today?" In order for the answers to that question to be positive and more correct, teachers can spend a few minutes talking about the day, and then writing down a few of the happenings. Talking about, writing, and then reading this journal entry makes the question of what they did each day easier for many kindergarten students to answer. It also gives the kindergarten teacher another opportunity to write for children before asking them to do this task.

Journal writing in kindergarten begins, for us, after the children have the opportunity to see the teacher think aloud and write. The first thing the teacher does is to write the date. Next, she discusses the events of the day. She may need to help her students organize the events in the correct order and decide about what to write, since you cannot write every detail of every day. Then, she writes these sentences on a large piece of chart paper. As she talks and writes, just like with the morning message, she says the words and spells them, writing the letters as she says them.

September 18

Today we began school with big group. Next, we heard a new story.

Then, we made a page for our class book about colors. We went to

music with Miss Melody. After music we made patterns with colors

for math. We ended the day in centers. School is fun!

As she writes, the teacher talks about what she is doing and why she is doing the things she is doing.

"We begin our journal entry with the date, **September 18** (you can put the year, too.) **September**, capital S-e-p-t-e-m-b-e-r, **eighteenth**." The teacher writes a one and an eight as she says, 'Eighteenth.'

"My first sentence is about what we did today. '**Today we began school with big group.**' I start each sentence with a capital letter because sentences begin that way. **Today**, capital T-o-d-a-y, **we**, w-e, **began**, b-e-g-a-n **school**, s-c-h-o-o-l, **with**, w-i-t-h, **big**, b-i-g, **group**, g-r-o-u-p, **period**. A period goes at the end of the sentence."

"**Next, we heard a new story. Next**, n-e-x-t, **we**, w-e, **heard**, h-e-a-r-d, **a**, a, **new**, n-e-w, **story**, s-t-o-r-y, **period**. A period goes at the end of this sentence, too."

The teacher continues talking about what the class did at school today and writing down sentences, spelling the words as she writes them and talking about the capital letters and ending marks (punctuation), until she has a journal entry. Time often determines the length. When time is short, the teacher can write three to four sentences and then read them to the class.

Once your students get used to watching you think, talk, and write the journal entry at the end of the day, they may want to join in and help you compose. Later in the year, as with the morning message, the class journal entry may become interactive writing, where the students help with the composing and the writing.

Writing a journal entry at the end of the school day helps students to focus on the important things they did in school that day. To get your students ready to write (spell) words, model this skill for them daily during your journal entry. When you begin words like "music," "Miss Melody," or "math," remind the children that these words begin just like Michael's and Michelle's names begin—same sound, same letter. You should say something like, "This word begins like Michael (or Michelle or Mommy). We know that words that begin like Michael begin with an 'm.'" Stretch out the words as you say and spell them so the children can hear the sounds and then watch as you write the letters. When you write for children, you provide a model for writing. Later, when they are asked to write their own journal entries each day, they will know what is expected and how to do it.

Signs, Schedules, and Directions in Centers

Kindergarten teachers often put signs, schedules, or directions in their classrooms and centers. When teachers write these items they have another opportunity to write for children and to demonstrate that writing serves a purpose.

The teacher has just finished the Shared Reading of a predictable big book. The after-reading activity was to "do the book," and the teacher taped this activity and wants to put it in the Listening Center. She wants to put the directions for this activity in the center so that everyone knows what is expected when it is their turn in the Listening Center. First, the teacher gathers the students around her and begins writing on a piece of lined chart paper.

"We are going to make a sign for the Listening Center. The sign will tell us what to do when we are in the Listening Center, so I will write '**Listening Center'** at the top. Next, I will write the directions, so I will add that to my title. (She adds the word '**Directions**' to the title.) The directions tell you what to do when you go to the center and listen to this tape."

"**Number one** (the teacher writes a numeral one on the chart paper) **Find the tape.**" The teacher writes "Find the tape." beside the numeral one and draws a picture of the tape after the sentence. She explains that the tape may be in the tape recorder, or on the table where the headsets and books are kept. If it is in the tape recorder, they are to leave it there. If it is not in the tape recorder, the students are to put it there.

"**Number two** (she writes a numeral two on the chart paper) **Choose 1 person to work the tape recorder.**" The teacher explains that she knows they all can do this, but if they all try to do this at the same time, there may be a problem. Therefore, only one person should be responsible for this job and that person will turn on the tape recorder and adjust the volume.

"**Number three** (she writes a numeral three on the chart paper) **Put on the headphones.**" The teacher explains how they wipe the headphones with "baby wipes" to clean the headsets before they use them.

```
┌─────────────────────────────────────────────────────────┐
│              Listening Center Directions                  │
│                                                           │
│    1.      Find the tape.                                 │
│                                                           │
│    2.      Choose 1 person to work the tape recorder.     │
│                                                           │
│    3.      Put on the headphones.                         │
│                                                           │
│    4.      Listen to the tape.                            │
│                                                           │
│    5.      Listen to the tape and read along.             │
│                                                           │
└─────────────────────────────────────────────────────────┘
```

"**Number four** (the teacher writes a numeral four on the chart) **Listen to the tape.**" The teacher explains to the students that the first time they will listen to the tape—just listen.

"**Number five** (she writes a numeral five on the chart) **Listen to the tape and read along.**" The teacher explains how they will read along with the tape the second time using the little books that came with the big books.

When directions are written for the children and the teacher is writing in front of the class, the chance of the children understanding the directions are much greater. The children also get more information about the directions as the teacher talks and writes. As you write the directions, any questions your students have can be answered and any problems can be solved before the children enter the center for a new activity. Another bonus of this activity is that you do not need to make this sign before school, after school, or during your "duty free" or "prep" time. This results in more learning for your students and less time spent getting ready, so just do it together!

How Writing For Children Is Multilevel

Writing for children can teach them what writing is, why people write, and how people write. For those students who are further along in their literacy journey, writing for children is important, too. When the teacher thinks as she writes, talking about what she will say and how she will write down her thoughts, she is modeling many skills (sentence structure, capitalization, punctuation, etc.) that are appropriate for the more advanced students. The open-ended questions the teacher asks after completing the writing ("What do you notice about this journal entry?") lead different students to notice different things, depending on their literacy levels. What the teacher talks about and how much she interacts with the students changes over the months as students do more and more of the work and the writing becomes interactive.

Morning messages, class signs, and class journals provide a teacher with opportunities to show children how people write and why they write. When a teacher writes for children, some of the students are learning that what you say, you can write, while other children are learning that you write from left to right and top to bottom, just like in reading. Still other children are learning that words start with capital letters, and sentences end with a period, exclamation mark, or a question mark. Other children are learning how to stretch out words, listen for the sounds they hear, and then write the letters that represent those sounds.

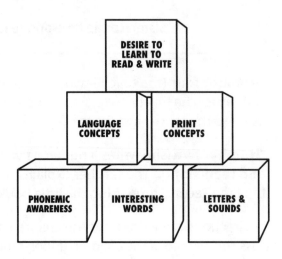

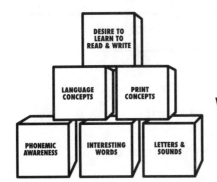

Chapter 6
Writing with Children

Writing with children is often called Shared Writing, and sometimes called interactive writing. It is usually done with students in the primary grades. During Shared Writing, the teacher and students compose together and talk about the writing as they write. The teacher may ask questions to clarify the meaning of the message, talk about the purpose, or discuss the intended audience. Sometimes she even invites the students to share the pen (or marker) by writing the parts they can. Writing with young students benefits them because they not only see the teacher think and write, they also have an opportunity to join in the thinking and writing with her. For some students, Shared Writing is the critical link between watching adults write and becoming independent writers.

In this chapter, we will share with you a number of ways to write with your students in kindergarten. Writing morning messages with the children's help, using interactive charts, and using predictable charts (formerly called "structured language experience") are all ways kindergarten teachers write with children.

Morning Messages

During the second half of the kindergarten year, the morning message changes from "writing for children" to "writing with children," as the students begin to share the writing, with or without sharing the pen. When young children write, it is often a difficult task for them if their fine motor skills are not well developed. When fine motor skills are not well developed, it takes some children a very long time to form the letters and to write words. Some kindergarten teachers feel that waiting for children to write the words takes too much time, and while waiting, other students have trouble staying on task. When kindergarten teachers feel this way, they should continue to write, but they should let their students do the talking as they do the writing.

Here is a morning message written later in the school year:

> Dear Class,
>
> Did March come in like a lion?
>
> We will talk about air and wind today.
>
> We will make kites in art.
>
> Love,
>
> Miss Williams

The teacher asks the children to help her write the greeting,

"If we begin with '**Dear Class,**' what do I write first? That's right. **Dear**, capital D-e-a-r. What do I write next? Right again. **Class**, capital C-l-a-s-s, **comma**." The children answer quickly. They have seen the teacher do this over one hundred times!

"Did March come in like a lion?" The teacher says each word as she writes it. "**Did…March…come…in…like…a…lion…question mark.**" She puts a question mark at the of this sentence.

The teacher and the class discuss that if the weather is nice, people say March came in like a lamb. If the weather is windy or stormy, people say March came in like a lion. She points out that she used a question mark at the end of her sentence because she asked a question. Next, the teacher and the class discuss the weather and the wind, and then answer the question in the message by saying, "March came in like a lamb."

"I am going to tell you something in the next sentence, '**We will talk about air and wind today.**'" The teacher asks, "Can anyone spell the first word 'we'?" Several children raise their hands, and the teacher writes what they say, "Capital W-e."

"Can anyone spell (or write) 'will'?" Several children again proudly raise their hands. When one student is called on he says, "w–i–l–l." This is not a difficult task at this time of the year because the teacher has been writing "we" and "will" on the morning message most days.

"My fourth sentence today is, '**We will make kites in art.**' Who can help me with this sentence?" The students say that it begins just like sentence three and tell the teacher to write, "We, Capital W-e, will, w-i-l-l."

Next, the teacher asks how to write the word "make" and calls on someone who, once again, spells it correctly!

"Can anyone help me with the word '**kites**'?" When the teacher notices some children looking at the word "kite" on the bulletin board, she calls on one of these children and brags on how smart he is when he answers her correctly.

"The next word is easy, it is the word **in**, i-n. Our next word is **art**. Who can find the word '**art**' in the room?" When a child looks on a chart with the specials listed, the teacher calls on that child to help her.

"How do I end my morning message? Yes, **Love**, capital L-o-v-e, **comma**-pause." She then writes her name, **Miss Williams**, as all the children say her name!

As the teacher continues writing morning messages for the remainder of the school year, she will work on these skills:

- What I say, I can write

- Stretching out words and listening for letter sounds

- Capitalization

- Punctuation

- Spelling high-frequency words

- Finding the interesting words in other places in the room, such as "lamb" in the writing center, "air" in the science center, etc.

- Finding rhyming words

- Finding words that begin alike

As the year advances, the teacher does less of the work and lets the children do more and more of the composing and writing of the morning message. "How do I start my morning message?" "Who can tell me the letters I need to write, 'Dear Class'?" "What do you think we will do today? Yes, you are right, we will work on our Mother's Day gifts today. Help me write that sentence." By this time of the kindergarten year, there are a few children in the class who can correctly spell most high-frequency words. The children are also able to hear the letter sounds and write the letters those sounds represent if the teacher allows them to stretch out the words with her.

As the teacher finishes the message, she continues to let the children do the talking, tell her what to write, or do the writing themselves. On some days, the children are doing all the work and spelling all the words correctly! Young children need to be shown how to write, and then be allowed to practice this skill daily. The morning message is a time when you teach children many things. You teach them how to think as they write, how to look in the classroom for words they do not know, how to use capitalization and correct punctuation just like they see in books, etc. When a teacher shows young students how she thinks as she writes, many children follow the model and also think as they write. The result is a marvelous morning message of which any kindergarten teacher and her class can be proud.

Dear Class,

> We will work on our Mother's Day gifts today.
>
> Your mothers will be surprised!
>
> What makes your mother so special?
>
> Today you will write a story about you mother.

Love,

Miss Williams

Interactive Charts

Interactive charts provide young children with the opportunity to manipulate text and interact with print. These charts also help transfer oral language skills to written language. An interactive chart can be based on a nursery rhyme, a familiar poem, song, or finger play, or something else that the students are learning about. The first thing the teacher does is to write the chart and then read it to the children. The first reading, and possibly the second and third readings, are just for enjoyment. Repeated readings of the chart help young students remember the words if the chosen text has rhythm and rhyme to support memorization. As emergent learners, children are active and concrete learners who need a lot of support, which interactive charts can provide. The charts also help children begin to match oral words with written text and provide children with the opportunity to learn how to self-check and self-correct. As children read these charts and gain control over printed words, they develop an "I can read" attitude.

The steps to making an interactive chart are quite simple:

1. Write a song, poem, or fingerplay on sentence strips, one strip per sentence.

   Four lines is an appropriate length for kindergarten. Always use your best printing so that your students will have a nice, neat model for handwriting. Be aware of the size, formation, and spacing of your writing.

2. Place these sentence strips in a pocket chart, or write the cha[rt on] chart paper.

3. Choose a part of the sentence strip for the children to manipulate— a rhyming word, a number word, etc. When using sentence stri[ps in a] pocket chart, the manipulated part can be placed in the pocket at [the cor]rect spot.

Here Are Some Examples of Interactive Charts:
Five Little Monkeys Jumping on the Bed
After reading *Five Little Monkeys Jumping on the Bed*, a lively, traditional rhyme re-told by Eileen Christelow (Clarion Books, 1989), the teacher might make an interactive chart with the repetitive part of the text. The chart would look like this:

Five Little Monkeys

[Five] little monkeys jumping on the bed.

One fell off and bumped his head.

Momma called the doctor and the doctor said,

"No more monkeys jumping on the bed!"

After the teacher reads the chart with the children, she changes the number word from five to four, and then the teacher and class read this verse together.

[Four] little monkeys jumping on the bed.

One fell off and bumped his head.

Momma called the doctor and the doctor said,

"No more monkeys jumping on the bed!"

After the teacher reads the chart with the children, she changes the number word from four to three, and then the teacher and class read this verse together.

[Three] little monkeys jumping on the bed.

One fell off and bumped his head.

Momma called the doctor and the doctor said,

"No more monkeys jumping on the bed!"

After the teacher reads the chart with the children, she changes the number word from three to two, and then the teacher and class read this verse together.

[Two] little monkeys jumping on the bed.

One fell off and bumped his head.

Momma called the doctor and the doctor said,

"No more monkeys jumping on the bed!

After the teacher reads the chart with the children, the teacher changes the number word from two to one, and then they read this verse together.

[One] little monkey jumping on the bed.

He fell off and bumped his head.

Momma called the doctor and the doctor said,

"No more monkeys jumping on the bed!"

The word that is manipulated in this example is the number word [five]. The teacher makes the word cards [four], [three], [two], and [one] so that the children can manipulate the number words and read the chart. By using this interactive chart, the children can see that almost all the words are the same, only the number word changes. When this chart is put in the Reading Center, children can continue to "read" the chart and practice this new skill.

Getting to Know You

Most Buildings Blocks teachers begin the year with some get-acquainted activities. The teacher focuses on a special child each day (see Chapter 8). Some teachers focus on the child's name the first time they do this activity with the class. The second time around the teacher may want to write an interactive chart and change the students' names and information daily to reflect what each student has to say about himself.

```
Getting to Know You

My name is _____.

I am _____ years old.

I like to eat _____.

I like to _____.
```

(See the "Getting to Know You" chart in CD-2505 Building Blocks "Plus" for Kindergarten package.)

Each day the teacher interviews the special student of the day and writes the four interactive pieces. The first thing she writes is the student of the day's name. Next, the child tells how old he is. Then, he tells his favorite food, and finally, he tells a word or two about what he likes to do. As the child dictates the words for each sentence, the teacher writes them down and then reads the sentence back to the class. This may be done in a pocket chart and rewritten on chart paper, or just written on chart paper so that the child can illustrate his sentences, and they can be displayed on a bulletin board or wall. Children are proud when they can read their own chart to family members and friends.

Interactive Charts and Themes

Later in the school year, teachers can tie into themes also. In the spring, when children are learning about plants and planting, it is a good time to make another interactive chart. This one is not based on a song, rhyme, or poem, but on something they are learning about—plants. The children can help the teacher with the word cards as they review what they have learned about plants.

```
Plants

In spring we see plants.

I will plant _____.

I will need a _____.

Plants need _____.
```

For the second sentence, the children have a choice to plant a favorite flower or vegetable. Let them name some flowers and vegetables (tulips, pansies, daisies, carrots, beans, radishes, etc.), write the words on sentence strips, and cut them apart for the chart. Teach your students to use the beginning sound and the pictures you have drawn to help read these words. For the next sentence, the students have to think about what will they need for planting. Let the children tell you what they have learned about planting, and what materials they will need for planting (seeds, a spade, a shovel, or a hoe). Finally, the children need to tell you what plants need to grow (good soil, sunshine, water, etc.).

Place this chart in a Science Center, so the children can manipulate the text and review these new concepts. Drawing pictures on the word cards helps young children find the right words and cross-check the oral word with both the picture and the beginning letters in the text; it also helps them look at word length. It is fun for the children to read this chart over and over again with different sentences each time they read it! There is a book devoted to interactive charts that many kindergarten teachers find helpful. It is called *Building Literacy with Interactive Charts* by Kristin Schlosser and Vickie Phillips (Scholastic, 1992).

Predictable Charts

We do a special kind of Shared Writing that was once called "structured language experience" (Cunningham, 1997), but is now called "predictable charts." We read predictable books so that emergent readers can experience success; why not write predictable charts so emergent writers can experience success? A predictable chart has a predictable pattern: I see…, I like…, My friend is…, etc. Sentence after sentence begins the same way on the chart and ends with the child's name who dictated the sentence in parentheses. *Month-by-Month Reading and Writing for Kindergarten* (Hall and Cunningham, 1997) contains "easy" predictable charts beginning in October.

After reading *Things I Like* by Anthony Browne, you can have the children finish the sentence "I like _____."

After reading *The Little Engine That Could* by Watty Piper (Grossett and Dunlap, 1978), you could have the children finish the sentence "I can _____."

After talking about colors and being introduced to color words, the predictable charts begins, "My favorite color is _____." (For this chart, the teacher writes the sentence with the student's favorite color marker!)

At Thanksgiving, after reading and talking about this special day, you can write a predictable chart, "I am thankful for _____."

After a field trip to a farm or a museum, a popular predictable chart is. "I saw a _____."

Five-Day Cycle for Predictable Charts

Ideas for predictable charts come from things that are happening in the classroom. Many teachers find a five-day cycle works well for each predictable chart made with the class.

Day 1 and 2: Dictation of the Sentences

The students are given a model or a pattern to follow by the teacher. The children dictate their sentences using the model provided, and the teacher writes each sentence on a large piece of chart paper, putting the child's name in parentheses at the end. After the dictation of each sentence, the teacher lets the child who dictated the sentence read the sentence back as she points to the words. Dictating the sentences and writing the chart often takes one day for a small class and two days if the class is large.

Day 3: Touch Reading the Sentences and Matching Words

On the third day, the teacher asks each student to "touch read" his sentence on the chart. She makes sure to move the chart to the student's eye level so he can easily read his sentence and does not have to stretch or crouch down for this task. Touching each word helps children learn to track print. Sometimes the teacher asks the children to find the longest and shortest words in their sentences, or she talks about the capital letters and punctuation. Another activity the teacher does, once she has made several charts, is to give the children their cut-up sentences in clear, resealable plastic bags. The teacher then calls on two or three of the children to match their cut-up sentences to their written sentences on the predictable chart. The children place the words in a pocket chart and compare the order of the cut-up words to the order of the words in the sentences on the chart.

Once the class has seen this modeled by a student, sometimes with the teacher's help, they will all be asked to arrange the words in their cut-up sentences to match their sentences on the predictable chart. While the children are doing this, the teacher walks around the room, monitors, helps the students who need it, and listens to the children read their sentences after matching them with the predictable chart.

Day 4: Sentence Builders

On the fourth day, the teacher focuses on the sentence, the words, the sounds of letters, and the letters. Before the lesson, the teacher uses sentence strips to write three sentences from the chart. She makes sure to include the name of the child who dictated the sentence. She cuts the words apart and puts them in an envelope or plastic baggie so that they are ready to use. The teacher uses one sentence at a time and passes out the words to as many children as she has words, making sure to give the name card to the child whose sentence they are going to build. The students are then asked to be "sentence builders." This means they come up to the front of the room, get themselves in the right places in the sentence, and show their words to the class. Some students know their words and can do this task quite easily. Other students have to match the word they are holding to the chart and count words to find their right place. Children often help each other find the right place for each word in the sentence. The child who is holding the card with his name usually knows that his place is at the end of the sentence! Finally, the teacher stands behind the sentence builders and touches each child as she reads the sentence with the class. She repeats this process for the other two cut-up sentences.

Once the students are used to "sentence builders," the teacher begins to ask questions about the sentences. "Can you find a certain word?" "Can you find a word that starts like 'Mommy'?" "Can you find a word that rhymes with 'ball'?" "Can you find a word that begins with 'b'?"

Day 5: Making a Class Book

The teacher begins by letting each child read his sentence from the chart, and then she lets the class read the chart together with her. She gives each child his cut-up sentence. (She made sure to prepare these ahead of time!) Each child puts the words from his sentence in the correct order and glues them along the bottom of a page. Next, the students will illustrate their sentences. The teacher makes a book cover and staples the book together. Now the students have a class big book to treasure all year! As the year progresses, the teacher gives the sentence strips to the students and lets them cut the words in their sentences apart. She may also mix up the words in the sentences so the students have to cut the words apart as well as paste them in the right order. She may also let them copy or type their sentences for books. The more the children learn, the more work the teacher can give them to do!

Examples of Predictable Charts

Names

At the beginning of this chapter we mentioned some of the popular, easy predictable charts. One of the easiest charts to begin with is, "My name is _____." Teachers usually start the year by doing some get-acquainted activities and learning the students' names. For this example, the teacher writes "Names" at the top of the chart. The first sentence she writes is "My name is Miss Williams." Then, the teacher calls on the student of the day to tell the class what his name is. Steve says, "My name is Steve." The teacher writes the words as Steve says them. Next, the teacher calls on another student who answers, "My name is Tracy." One by one, the children use this model and complete the sentence with their names.

The finished chart looks like this:

Names

My name is <u>Miss Williams</u>.

My name is <u>Steve</u>.

My name is <u>Tracy</u>.

My name is <u>Janet.</u>

My name is <u>Mandy</u>.

My name is <u>Corey</u>.

My name is <u>Patty</u>.

My name is <u>Julie</u>.

My name is <u>Chris</u>.

My name is <u>John</u>.

My name is <u>José.</u>

My name is <u>Mary</u>.

My name is <u>Angelica</u>.

My name is <u>Hannah</u>.

My name is <u>David</u>.

My name is <u>Chad</u>.

My name is <u>Shawn</u>.

My name is <u>Jamarcio</u>.

My name is <u>Susan</u>.

My name is <u>Sally</u>.

My name is <u>Eleanor</u>.

My name is <u>Julio</u>.

My name is <u>Kristen</u>

My name is <u>Karen</u>.

My name is <u>Matthew</u>.

Day 1 and 2: Dictation of the sentences

The teacher talks about the names of the students in her class. She begins her predictable chart with the sentence, "My name is _____ ." She finishes this sentence the first time with her name. After writing her sentence first on the predictable chart, she reads it back to the class. Next, she asks the students to tell her the rest of the sentences. Each child says, "My name is…" and completes the sentence with his name. As each child dictates his sentence, the teacher writes it on the chart. Writing the chart will take one day (sometimes two days if you have a large class).

Day 3: Touch Reading the Sentences

On the third day, the teacher asks each student to "touch read" his sentence on the chart. Each child reads, "My name is…" and says his name. The teacher and the class start at the top of the chart and read to the bottom. Each child takes a turn. The teacher knows she has a few children that need a little extra help and does not call on them at the beginning. After a few sentences, they pick up the pattern and then everyone can be successful at this task.

Day 4: Sentence Builders

On the fourth day, the teacher focuses on the sentences, the words, the sounds of letters, and the letters. Before the lesson, the teacher uses sentence strips to write three sentences from the chart. The names of the children who dictated the sentences are included in parentheses at the end of the sentences. She cuts the words apart and puts them in an envelope or plastic baggie so they are ready for use in class. The teacher uses one sentence at a time and passes out the words to four children, making sure to give the name card to the child whose sentence the children are going to build. The students are then asked to be "sentence builders." To do this correctly, the child holding "My" has to be at the beginning of the sentence. The next place in line belongs to the child holding "name." In the third place is the child holding the word "is." The last spot belongs to the child holding his name. Finally, the teacher stands behind the "sentence builders" and touches each child as she reads the sentence with the class. The teacher repeats this process for the other two cut-up sentences.

Day 5: Making a Class Book

| Names |
| by |
| Miss |
| Williams's |
| Class |

For this predictable chart, the teacher writes the sentences from the chart on drawing paper and lets the children add their handwritten names to the sentences, "My name is _____". In this example, the children do not have to put the words in the correct order or glue the words at the bottom of a page. All the children have to do is illustrate their sentences with their self-portraits once they have written their names. To finish the book, the teacher makes a front cover, including the title, and a plain back cover. Then, she staples the pages inside in the order they appear on the chart. Now the students have a class big book with all the names of the students in their class. Some kindergarten students will be able to read each sentence, including the names of all the students. Other children will only be able to read their own sentences. Still others will pick up the book and search for the page they did, looking for their name because it is the first word they can read. This class book, written by the children and including all their names and self-portraits, is a wonderful addition to any kindergarten classroom's Reading Center!

What You Do At a Sleepover

As a part of a kindergarten theme on "Nighttime Stories," the teacher reads the class *Ira Sleeps Over* by Bernard Waber. Next, she plans a sleepover for her class (this can be real or imaginary). Then, she poses a question to her class, "What do you do at a sleepover?" After much discussion, the class decides to make a list of things they can do at a sleepover. The teacher uses a predictable chart to list what each child has to say.

What You Can Do At a Sleepover

You can read stories. (Miss Williams)

You can tell stories. (Steve)

You can eat snacks. (Tracy)

You can eat candy! (Mandy)

You can color. (John)

You can play video games. (Corey)

You can eat junk food. (Janet)

You can stay up until midnight. (Julie)

You can sleep! (Patty)

You can watch movies. (José)

You can drink hot chocolate. (Sally)

You can hear music. (Angelica)

You can do what you want. (Hannah)

You can roast marshmallows. (David)

You can watch T.V. (Chad)

You can read books. (Paul)

You can dance. (Shawn)

You can stay up late. (Karen)

You can play games. (Kristen)

You can eat pizza. (Susan)

You can sleep with a teddy bear. (Matthew)

You can sleep with a stuffed animal. (Eleanor)

You can play with toy cars. (Jamarcio)

Day 1 and 2: Dictation of the Sentences

The teacher reads the book and talks about sleepovers with her class. "Have you ever slept over at somebody's house?" "What did you do?" "What did you take with you?" "Where did you sleep?" "Were you scared?" Because she has a large class (more than 15 students), the teacher begins the sentence dictation and writing of the chart on the first day and finishes this task on the second day. If she had been lucky enough to have a small number of students, she could have read and discussed on the first day and had the children dictate their sentences on the second day.

Day 3: Touch Reading the Sentences and Matching

On the third day, the teacher asks the students to "touch read" their sentences on the chart. The teacher lets the children use a special pointer with a gold star at the end to point to the words as they read their sentences. The teachers tells the students to pretend they are reading at night by starlight! (What fun!) Each child reads, "You can..." and then tells how he or she finished the sentence. The teacher and the class start at the top of the chart and read to the bottom, with each child taking a turn. If the teacher knows that some children need a little extra help, she does not call on them at the beginning, but waits until near the end. After a few sentences, most children can pick up the pattern and be successful.

Day 4: Sentence Builders

Today, the teacher focuses on the sentences, the words, the sounds of letters, and the letters. Before the lesson, the teacher uses three sentence strips to write three sentences from the chart. The names of the children who dictated the sentences are included in parentheses at the end of the sentences. She cuts the words apart and puts them in an envelope or plastic bag, ready to use in class. The teacher uses one sentence at a time and passes out the words to some of the children, making sure to give the name card to the child whose sentence they are going to build. The students are then asked to be "sentence builders." Finally, the teacher stands behind the "sentence builders" and touches each child as she reads the sentence with the class. The teacher repeats this process for the other two cut-up sentences.

Day 5: Making a Class Book

| What You
Can Do at a
Sleepover
by
Miss Williams's
Class

For this activity, the children get their own sentences with the words from their sentences cut apart. Next, each child has to put the words from his sentence in the correct order. Then, the teacher checks each sentence, and finally, the students glue the words along the bottoms of their pages. When the sentences are correctly glued to the pages, the students illustrate their sentences. To finish the book the teacher makes a front cover, including the title, *What You Can Do at a Sleepover,* and a plain back cover. She staples the pages inside in the order they appear on the chart. Now the students have another class book to put in the Reading Center or to read on another day while having a "pretend sleepover" with the class!

Good Food

During a health theme on "Foods That Are Good for You," a kindergarten teacher reads the book, *Gregory, the Terrible Eater* by Mitchell Sharmat (Simon & Schuster, 1980). This leads to a class discussion of foods that are good for you and foods that are not good for you. Then, the teacher begins a predictable chart about good food to eat. She titles the chart, "Good Food," and then writes, "_____ is/are good to eat." After the children have dictated their sentences, this is what the finished chart looks like:

Good Food

Cheese is good to eat. (Miss Williams)

Carrots are good to eat. (Susan)

Watermelon is good to eat. (Chris)

Oranges are good to eat. (Steve)

Raisins are good to eat. (Janet)

Celery is good to eat. (Tracy)

Chicken is good to eat. (Mandy)

Apples are good to eat. (Julie)

Bananas are good to eat. (Corey)

Salad is good to eat. (Patty)

Spaghetti is good to eat. (Eleanor)

Broccoli is good to eat. (José)

Cauliflower is good to eat. (Sally)

Tomatoes are good to eat. (Angelica)

Vegetables are good to eat. (Hannah)

Soup is good to eat. (Shawn)

Chili is good to eat. (Jamarcio)

Fish is good to eat. (Chad)

Pizza is good to eat. (Karen)

Macaroni and cheese is good to eat. (Kristen)

Tacos are good to eat. (Julio)

Blueberries are good to eat. (David)

Strawberries are good to eat. (Matthew)

Day 1 and 2: Dictation and Writing the Sentences

The teacher reads the book *Gregory, the Terrible Eater,* or *Eating the Alphabet,* or any other book about foods that are nutritious. She is planning to bring in some of her favorite foods (little carrots, tender celery, dry roasted peanuts, fresh strawberries, etc.) and has asked her students' parents to send a favorite healthy snack to school. She cuts the fresh fruits and vegetables in small pieces for a tasting party. The teacher talks about her favorite "healthy" foods, staying away from foods that are too sugary or too fatty. When two children say french fries and candy are their favorite foods, she reminds them that those foods are not "nutritious," because they contain too much fat or too much sugar. A wonderful resource for this theme and chart is the book, *Kinder Krunchies, Healthy Snack Recipes for Children* by Karen S. Jenkins (Discovery Toys Inc., 1997). The book is full of wonderful recipes like delicious dip, nutty numbers, etc. Make one recipe each day for a snack while studying healthy foods and working on this predictable chart.

Begin the sentence dictation and writing of the chart on the first day and finish this task on the second day. The children tell the teacher something healthy that they like to eat and they complete the sentence, "_____ is good to eat."

Day 3: Touch Reading the Sentences and Matching

On the third day the teacher asks each student to "touch read" his sentence on the chart. The teacher lets the children finger point to each word in their sentences as they read them. This is an easy task for the sentence, "Cheese is good to eat," but it is a harder task when the sentence has the word carrots or strawberries in it. Young children want to point to a word for each sound they hear. They get confused until they realize that "big" words have lots of letters and more than one sound.

The teacher and the class start reading at the top of the chart and read to the bottom. Each child takes a turn reading his/her own sentence. When she has children that need a little extra help, the teacher does not call on them for a sentence at the beginning of the chart, but waits until near the end. After watching a few children dictate their sentences to the teacher, watching the teacher write the sentences on the predictable chart, and then reading the sentences themselves, most children pick up the pattern and are successful. When "touch reading" is easy for the students, the teacher will use the cut-up sentences for tomorrow's lesson to do some "matching" today. At this time, all the students take their cut-up sentences (which the teacher or assistant has prepared ahead of time) and go back to their desks and match the words in their cut-up sentence to the words on the chart. By using the sentences on the predictable chart as a model, most children can do this task. The teacher's job is to circulate, help when needed, and show the children how to use the chart to self-check and self-correct. She should also listen to the children read the sentences they have built on their desks.

Day 4: Sentence Builders

On the fourth day, the teacher focuses on the sentences, the words, the sounds of letters, and the letters. Before the lesson, the teacher uses three sentence strips to write three sentences from the chart. The names of the children who dictated the sentences are included in parentheses at the end of the sentences. She cuts the words apart and puts them in an envelope ready to use in class. The teacher uses one sentence at a time and passes out the words to some of the children, making sure to give the name card to the child whose sentence she is going to build. The students are asked to be "sentence builders." The teacher stands behind the "sentence builders" and touches each child as she reads the sentence with the class. The teacher repeats this process for the other two cut-up sentences.

Day 5: Making a Class Book

For this activity, the children get their own sentences. The words from their sentences are cut apart. Next, each child has to put the words from his sentence in the correct order. Then, the teacher checks each sentence, and finally, the students glue the words along the bottoms of their pages. When the sentences are correctly glued to the pages, the students illustrate their sentences. To finish the book, the teacher makes a front cover, including the title, *Good Food,* and a plain back cover. She staples the pages inside in the order they appear on the chart. Now the students have added another class book to the Reading Center!

How We Use Water

April is known as the rainy month. During April, many teachers talk about rain and water. Kindergarten children are amazed by all the different ways that people use water. They like to learn that they can write H_2O and it means water! On the next page is a predictable chart one teacher came up with for water usage.

How We Use Water

You need water to wash clothes. (Miss Williams)

You need water to drink. (Eleanor)

You need water to wash your hair. (Mandy)

You need water to make tea. (Susan)

You need water to wash the car. (Steve)

You need water to water the garden. (Tracy)

You need water to water flowers. (Patty)

You need water to make lemonade. (Sally)

You need water to water the lawn. (Janet)

You need water to cook with. (Hannah)

You need water to wash your face. (Mary)

You need water to brush your teeth. (John)

You need water to wash the dog. (Paul)

You need water to water the grass. (Julio)

You need water to make punch. (Karen)

You need water to live. (Angelica)

You need water to put in bottles. (Jamarcio)

You need water to swim. (Chad)

You need water to take a shower. (Shawn)

You need water to make ice. (Corey)

You need water to wash the dishes. (Jamarcio)

You need water to fill up a pool. (Matthew)

Day 1 and 2: Dictation and Writing the Sentences

The teacher in this example is using a week in April to help children learn about rain, water, and even the water cycle. She begins the sentence dictation and writing of the chart on the first day of the week she is talking and teaching about water, and finishes this task on the second day. Each child tells the teacher one way that he knows that people use water. Their sentences read, "You need water to _____."

Day 3: Touch Reading the Sentences and Matching

On the third day, the teacher asks each student to "touch read" his or her sentence on the chart. The teacher lets the children point to each word in their sentences as they read them. By this time of the year, "touch reading" is an easy task for many of the students so the teacher will use the cut-up sentences for tomorrow's lesson to do some "matching" today. The children use their sentences from the predictable chart as their models. The teacher circulates, helps when needed, and listens to the children as they read their sentences.

Day 4: Sentence Builders

On the fourth day, the teacher focuses on the sentences, the words, the sounds of letters, and the letters. Before the lesson, the teacher uses three sentence strips to write three sentences from the chart. The names of the children who dictated the sentences are included in parentheses at the end of the sentences. She cuts the words apart and puts them in an envelope, ready to use in class. The teacher uses one sentence at a time and passes out the words to some of the children, making sure to give the name card to the child whose sentence they are going to build. The students are asked to be "sentence builders." The teacher stands behind the "sentence builders" and touches each child as she reads the sentence with the class. The teacher repeats this process for the other two cut-up sentences.

Day 5: Making a Class Book

How We Use Water by Miss Williams's Class

For this activity, the children get their own sentences. The words from their sentences are cut apart. Next, each child has to put the words from his sentence in the correct order. Then, the teacher checks each sentence, and finally, the students glue the words along the bottoms of their pages. When the sentences are correctly glued to the pages, the students illustrate their sentences. To finish the book the teacher makes a front cover, including the title, *How We Use Water,* and a plain back cover. She staples the pages inside in the order they appear on the chart. Once again, the students have added another class-made book to the Reading Center!

How Writing with Children Is Multilevel

Interactive morning messages, interactive charts, and predictable charts are multilevel because children work at their own levels. When children are writing a morning message with the teacher, some of them are learning that what they say, they can write. Other students are learning to read what the teacher has written. Still other students are learning how to spell words and punctuate sentences. When writing interactive charts with the teacher, some children are learning the rhyme or refrain. Other children are learning that changing words can make a new song or poem. Some other children are learning how to read, and possibly how to write, all the words. When the students dictate new words to the teacher, see the teacher write these words down on paper, and then "read" the words back to the teacher, all of them understand more about reading and writing. Interactive writing, with or without sharing the pen, and predictable charts are examples of writing with children. These activities provide additional opportunities for all kindergarten students to see themselves as readers and writers.

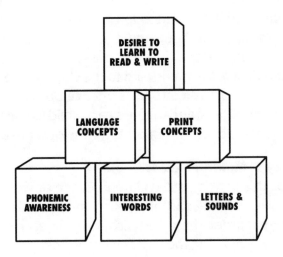

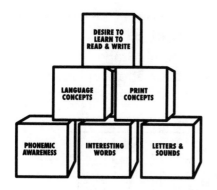

Chapter 7
Writing by Children

Now that your kindergarten students have had the opportunity to see you write daily (Chapter 5), and you have done some shared writing that included predictable charts (Chapter 6), you will find that most of your students are ready to write by themselves. To help teachers understand what is happening and what their students know about writing, we always refer teachers to J. Richard Gentry's work on the stages of spelling (writing) development. In Gentry's article for *Early Years K-8* (May 1985) titled, "You Can Analyze Developmental Spelling—And Here's How To Do It!," he explains the five stages of spelling development that children go through and tells what happens to young children and why it happens in each stage. Children's writing attempts are no longer considered "mistakes," but a mirror into what children know about words and how they represent that word knowledge. In Gentry's first two books, *Spel Is a Four Letter Word* (Heinemann, 1987) and *Teaching Kids to Spell* with Jean Wallace Gillet (Heinemann, 1993), he explains the five stages of spelling/writing development. By reading these books you can get a better understanding of how young children learn to spell and write. All children go through these five stages, but at different ages and for different lengths of time. A young child's writing and spelling, as well as an older child's writing and spelling, tells a teacher what that child knows about words and what phonics he can use when he writes.

Gentry writes that if a teacher is aware of children's developmental spelling progress, it will enable her to respond intelligently when working with students. During writing time in kindergarten, a teacher has the opportunity to both respond to and "coach" the students so that they can become better writers as they learn more about words and more about writing. A teacher's daily instruction and the activities she uses should depend on her looking at her students' work and discovering what they already know and what they need to learn next.

Stages of Writing/Spelling Development
Stage 1: The Precommunicative or Pre-phonemic Stage
This is the stage before children know much about letters and sounds (phonemes). Spelling and writing at this stage consist of scribbles and random letters. See the examples below:

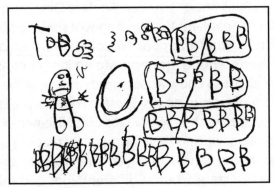

Stage 2: The Semiphonetic Stage
The second stage can be seen when words begin to be represented by a letter or two. The letters these young children write are usually the first letters they hear in a word or the first and last letter. See the example below:

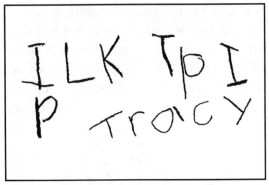

I like to play. I play. Tracy

Stage 3: The Phonetic Stage

Vowels appear in the third stage, but not necessarily the right vowel. The long vowels appear correctly represented first, but there is an attempt at short vowel sounds, too. Regional accents often affect how vowels are represented. See the examples below:

I watched T. V.

I will play in the snow.

Stage 4: Transitional Stage

In this stage, the sounds are represented and the spelling is possibly an English spelling. When kindergarten children are bright and are allowed to write each day, they reach this stage quite quickly.

> Magnts can pic up pr kips. It
> will not pic up a cryon. Magnts
> are strg.
> Kevin

Magnets can pick up paper clips. It will not pick up a crayon. Magnets are strong.
Kevin

Stage 5: Correct Spelling

We have no kindergarten writing samples for Stage 5 because there are few five-year-olds who can spell all words correctly, unless they limit what they say to known spelling words! Kindergarten students can be seen going through the first four stages as they learn about words and use what they know in their daily writing.

The First Writing Lesson(s)

It is best to use plain paper for the first writing lessons with your kindergarten class because not all of your students will be ready to write on lined paper. You will have more success with your students if they are familiar with morning messages (writing <u>for</u> children) and predictable charts (writing <u>with</u> children) before they are asked to write by themselves.

The first writing lesson begins with the teacher talking about the ways in which people write. She tells her class,

"Some people use pictures when they write." (You can draw a smiling face on the board or on a piece of chart paper to illustrate this.)

"When teachers put smiling faces on papers they are saying, 'I like your work!'"

"Some people use pictures to help them say what they want to say. You can use pictures when you write if that will help you. If you want to say, 'I love my dog,' then you may want to draw a heart and a dog."

"When you read it you will say, 'I love my dog.'" (The teacher points to the heart as she says 'love' and the dog as she says 'dog'.)

"Some children make wavy lines and call it writing. They think about what they want to say and then write, 'I love my cat.' It looks something like this:

When children write like this they usually remember what they wanted to say. You can write like this if you want." (The teacher points to the scribbling as she says this).

"Another way children write is to use the letters and sounds they know. They stretch out words, and write down what they hear, such as 'I pl n m p.' They read this back, 'I play in my pool.' The letters help these children remember what they said."

I pl n m p

"Another way children write is to use some words they know. If you can write your name, then write it. If you can write 'cat' or 'dog' or 'Mom,' do it."

John cat Mom

"John can read his sentence, 'John has a cat and a Mom.' If you know some words you can use those words to help you write."

"Some people write just like I do when I write a chart or the morning message every day. They use words and write in sentences. When children do this, they think about what they want to tell the class, and then they stretch out the words and write them down as best they can.

I love to play outside.

If you want to use words and write sentences, you can do that."

"So, when you write about yourself today there are lots of ways you can do it: you can draw your picture, you can make some lines or letters, you can try some words you know, or you can write some sentences. Use what will help you to tell me something about you."

Here are four samples from a first writing lesson early in September in one kindergarten class:

Lydia - copies words in the room and adds family names

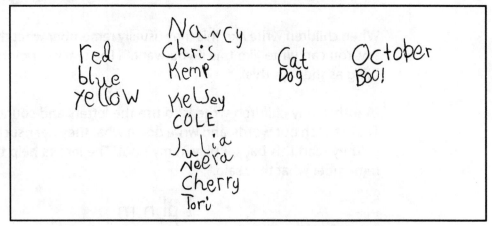

Nathan - draws pictures and squares; writes numbers, name

Julia - draws a picture of a cat and writes the word CAT

Katey - writes some words and names she finds in the room

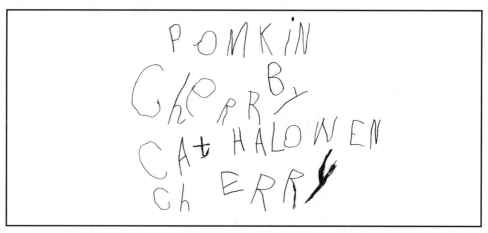

After observing the class, the teacher knows she will have to let the children watch her a little longer before she can begin daily writing. She allows them to copy in the writing center and use pencils, pens, and markers to write what they want on plain paper. She continues with her morning message, reading the room for words, and stretching out words.

Two Months Later

This is what the writing looked like two months later, using the same students who did the previous samples.

Lydia

I want it to snow a lot. I will build a snowman and I will catch snowflakes. I love the snow. I will throw snowballs at my mom and my dad.

Nathan

My dog just had puppies yesterday.

Julia

I got my hair cut. It is beautiful.

Katey

My mom helps my dad mow the grass.

What made the difference? The teacher claims that the morning message was a daily model, predictable charts helped children see that what they could say, they could write, and being able to coach some children when they were writing in the writing center helped her class move forward in writing.

Third Quarter

After the winter holidays the teacher begins to have her students write daily. She uses pieces of plain paper and a binding machine to make "writing journals" for her students' daily writing. Another teacher staples together several sheets of paper so her children can have a new booklet each month. Both of these teachers do a daily "mini-lesson" and then let the children write. At the end of their writing time, the children form a circle and several of them get to share their writing. Daily writing in a "journal" or notebook and coaching a few children each day at writing time paid off. Here are some examples of students' writing from the third quarter of the school year:

I got my fingernails painted. The color was red. My mom painted my nails.

If I had a pot of gold I would share it with everybody in the whole entire world.

I ply with cats. They ply wth me to. Thr nams ar Sugar Snoball and Honey. My favrt is Snoball becos she plys olit. I fed tham lonch.

I play with cats. They play with me, too. Their names are Sugar, Snowball, and Honey. My favorite is Snowball because she plays a lot. I feed them lunch.

End of the Year

By the end of the year, all the students are writing and reading their writing! Here are some samples that any kindergarten teacher would be proud to show off!

I whaet to Garhe. He whes a grat seegr. It whes luod. He had a lot av anogy. I had fun thaer. We had cande and a drek. We hrde Thresa Halewood. She had a grat vose. She whas drast up.

I went to Garth. He was a great singer. It was loud. He had a lot of energy. I had fun there. We had candy and a drink. We heard Trisha Yearwood. She had a great voice. She was dressed up.

My frnds play with me. My frnds like me.
My frnds do things with me. My friends love me.
My friends aru fun. My frnds can do things.
I can go to my frnds haws wan ivr I wit to.
I like my frnds. My frnds eat with me.
My frnds culr with me. My frnds run with me.
My frnds wich a ranbo with me. My frnds red with me.

My friends play with me. My friends like me. My friends do things with me. My friends love me. My friends are fun. My friends can do things. I can go to my friend's house whenever I want to. I like my friends. My friends eat with me. My friends color with me. My friends run with me. My friends watch a rainbow with me. My friends read with me.

My sestr is fun. We like to lafe.
She likes to play. She likes to sweig.
She likes to coler. She likes to coler with me.
I like to hold her. She has spineubether.
I slepe wite her. Sometimes she likes
to get in the pool.
My sister is funny. My sister loves me.
And I love her.
She is swete.

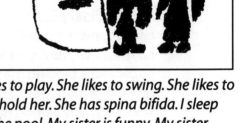

My sister is fun. We like to laugh. She likes to play. She likes to swing. She likes to color. She likes to color with me. I like to hold her. She has spina bifida. I sleep with her. Sometimes she likes to get in the pool. My sister is funny. My sister loves me. And I love her. She is sweet.

> Horsis ar important to me and Bailey. Me and Bailey like to rid horsis. My horsis is black. And baileys horsis is brown. Horsis are diffit from zebras because zebras have strips and horsis dot. I love horsis beus they ar cut. Y ou h ave to fed tham so they will bee a live. Win I gro up I will help horsis. Horsis are fun. horsis have babys. Horsis are pot of the farm grop. Wen I gro up me and Bailey will hlp horsis.

Horses are important to me and Bailey. Me and Bailey like to ride horses. My horse is black. And Bailey's horse is brown. Horses are different from zebras because zebras have stripes and horses don't. I love horses because they are cute. You have to feed them so they will be alive. When I grow up I will help horses. Horses are fun. Horses have babies. Horses are part of the farm group. When I grow up me and Bailey will help horses.

Daily Writing or "Journal Writing"

We usually recommend daily writing beginning in January. Why? Because by January your students have been in school almost half a year and have watched you write on numerous occasions. They have written for you and have grown in their word knowledge. Most students' attempts can be "read," and most students are using words now as well as pictures. The scribbles and random letters are beginning to disappear as the children stretch out words, hear the sounds, and remember the letters that make those sounds. Daily writing will now be a task most students can do!

Many Building Blocks teachers will staple together several sheets of plain paper each month so that the students can start with "January Journals," and they will have a new journal to write in each month. Other teachers use sheets of plain paper and a binding machine to make journals for their students to use during the remainder of the year. You can decide which format will work best for you and your students. Daily writing gives children an opportunity to use their knowledge of letters, sounds, and words to write, and then to read what they write. It is wonderful to see young children writing what they want to say, slowly saying words and listening for the letter sounds they have learned.

Coached Writing

Many young children need some individual help to become writers. Coached writing is when the teacher sits down with a child and "coaches," or helps, the child become a better writer. The coaching usually takes place during a special few minutes when one child has the teacher's undivided attention. When a teacher works individually with a student, she will, of course, get better writing out of that child than if the child is writing without help. If done correctly, coaching helps move students toward independence.

As the coaching session begins, if the child has not written anything the teacher will ask her what she is going to write about and what the first sentence is going to be. If the child has already started writing, the teacher asks her to read it aloud. The teacher "oohs" and "ahhs" over what the child has written and asks the child what she is going to say next. The teacher helps each child see that anything they want to tell, they can write. During the "coaching" conferences, the teacher helps the children write what they want to say by finding words they know in the room. She encourages them to slowly stretch out the words they do not know and cannot find by reading the room. They are coached to listen for the letter sounds that they know and write the letters representing those sounds.

"You want to write about your new bike. That's a good thing to write about! Tell me about your bike." (The child says, "My bike is red.")

"Let's write that. Say 'my'. What sounds do you hear? Write those sounds." (The child may write "mi.")

"What is the next word?" (The child says, "bike.") "Stretch out that word and write those sounds." (The child stretches out the word and says, "b-i- k" and writes the letters for the three sounds he hears.)

"My bike is…can you find the word 'is' on the morning message?" (The child looks on the morning message and writes "i-s.")

"What color is your bike?" (The child answers, "red.") "Can you find that with the color words?" (The child looks up at the color words on the wall and writes, "red.")

"Now, can you tell me something else about your bike?"

Invented Spelling

One of the main ways the teacher helps, or coaches, is by encouraging invented spelling. As children try to spell words, they should:

- say the word slowly

- listen to themselves saying sounds

- think about what they have learned about letters and sounds

This helps children develop their understanding of how sounds make up words. Invented spelling was never meant to be "anything goes." Its purpose is to free kids to write. When children depend on the teacher's help to spell every word correctly, they are unable to express themselves freely. When teachers encourage invented spelling, they are saying to children that they want them to do their best and spell words like they sound. Using invented spelling allows even kindergarten children to concentrate on their message and helps them see themselves as writers (Routman, 1996).

When children use invented spelling, they are using writing to communicate just like adults write to communicate. Invented spellers have discovered a system that is based on the same sound principles as conventional spelling, in which letters stand for sounds. What these young writers do not know yet are the fine points of how their spelling system differs from the conventional system. However, they have already learned the most important thing—what spelling is all about.

Invented spelling is phonics in use. When kindergarten students use invented spelling, they discover phonics on their own. When young children write, they learn the names of the letters of the alphabet and the sounds those letters make in words. They begin to pay attention to the sounds in words and to the sounds in the names of letters, then they put these two discoveries together. If a "d" sound is at the beginning of the word "dog," the beginning and end of "dad," and in the name of the letter "d," then maybe the letter "d" can be used to write the words "dog" and "dad."

When young children invent the spelling of words, they carefully analyze the words they want to write. They listen for individual sounds in words, usually in the correct sequence. They also review the letters they know, looking for one that can represent the sound(s) they have isolated, and then they write the letter. They repeat these steps as they move on to other sounds in a word and to other words in their writing. Young writers do not memorize their invented spelling. They do the "sound-by-sound" analysis of a word each time they write. Later, when they come to the point of using their memories for how words look, they will have plenty of conventional spelling models in books, on predictable charts, in the morning message each day, and in the print on the walls of their kindergarten classroom. However, invented spelling is not every child's preferred way of writing.

Some children are inclined right from the start to depend on how words look instead of sounding them out. Other children are perfectionists, but only a few. These children compare their first spelling attempts to conventional spelling and refuse to spell differently. They want to be right. They often ask for lots of help and need to be encouraged to take risks. If these children can learn to use "sound" or "ear spelling" along with letter knowledge, and learn to depend on themselves at least some of the time, they will make discoveries and learn more about how words work (Richels, 1993).

Invented spelling is a mirror into which a child looks to learn about words. When a teacher spells a word for a child, all the teacher knows is that the child cannot spell that word. When children are encouraged to write as best they can, the teacher can see the stages of spelling (writing) development. The teacher can also see what letters and sounds the children can hear, and know how they represent those sounds. These observations lead the teacher to see what else their students need to learn about letters and sounds. Watch and listen to children when they read and write. Do they know the names of many letters of the alphabet? When five-year-olds write "pla" for "play," "sno" for "snow," and "sre" for "sorry," teachers need to respond, "Good writing! I can read that!"

Mini-lessons by the Teacher

Showing children how to write and how people think as they write should be done daily in what is called a "mini-lesson." This short, five-minute lesson occurs at the start of writing time, just before the children are asked to write by themselves. The best way to show children how to write is to write for them. You can do this by modeling the writing of a short "story" or "piece" each day and let the students listen to you talk about your thinking process as they watch you write. The first thing you model is how to choose a topic from the many things you could write (tell) about.

"I think I will write about spring today. The sun is shining, the grass is turning green, plants are growing, and flowers are beginning to bloom. This would be a good day to write about spring. I could tell you so many things I see that remind me it's spring now. I could also tell about our new swing. That would be a good thing to write about! We just got the new swing over the weekend. It hangs from the back porch. We had to put wooden planks on the ground under the swing so we wouldn't drag our feet in the mud after it rains. Another thing I could write about today is the basketball game I watched last night. There was a big basketball game on television last night. Two college teams were playing for the national collegiate championship and lots of people around here watched that game. I watched that game, and I could tell you all about it."

Talking about the different things you could "tell about" and then write about helps children think of things they could "tell about" and then write about themselves. This really pays off for kindergarten teachers. As a matter of fact, it pays off for teachers at any grade level! Modeling how you think about what you could write, and then writing about those things, shows kids just what you expect them to do. The children follow the teacher's lead, and they choose a subject that interests them. It could be one you mentioned, one you wrote about, or something special that is happening to them. One little girl in Albuquerque wrote about how her family was planning to go visit her grandparents in Mexico. Everyone was going except her sister, who didn't have the right papers. What was important to her that day was whether or not her sister would be able to go on the family visit!

Talk as you write:

"For the first sentence, I will say, '**Today is warm and sunny.**' I can look at the pocket chart and see the words 'Today' and 'is' so I copy them and write them on my paper. I start with a capital 'T' because sentences start with a capital letter. 'Today is'… now I want to write, 'warm and sunny.' I look on the calendar board and I see the words 'warm' and 'sunny' so I can let the calendar board help with those two words. I put a period at the end of that sentence. The next thing I want to say is, '**The grass is green.**' The color words chart will help me write the word, 'green.' Then I will write, '**Plants are growing.**' Let me stretch the word 'Plants' out…capital P-l-a-n-t (write the letters as you stretch them out and say each one), are (write 'are'), growing…g-r-o-w-i-n-g (stretching the word and writing it also). Now I want to say, '**It feels like spring.**' It (write 'it'), feels (stretch that word out and write the letters as you say the sounds) f-e-e-l-s, like...I have written that word on charts many times, l-i-k-e, spring (once again, stretch it out and write the letters as you say the sounds) s-p-r-i-n-g. I think I will put an exclamation mark at the end because I get excited about all the things spring brings!"

The children will follow your lead by thinking about what they are going to write, stretching out words and writing the letters and sounds they hear, reading the room, finding words they want to write, and writing. Watch your students stretch out the words and write the letters for the sounds they hear. They will also be able to read their writing and so will you! As the children write, continue to praise their attempts, see who needs more individual help, and "coach" them so that they will become even better writers.

After a few mini-lessons where you do all the thinking and writing, continue to do your mini-lessons, but use a Shared Writing format where the children help you compose the story (write about subjects that are familiar to everyone), stretch out the words, and spell the words.

Don't Be an Editor, Be a Cheerleader!

We like to celebrate children's invented spelling and writing, while coaching them to become better writers and better spellers. When some young children write at home or in school, their parents tell them their writing is wonderful and prove it by posting it on the refrigerator, or a special bulletin board in the child's room. Sometimes these parents even bring their child's writing to work and "show it off" to friends and coworkers. Other times the parents will send the writing to grandma or grandpa, who will brag some more. These children have their own personal "cheerleaders." They develop self-esteem, and they believe they can write even though they are young. However, not all children are so fortunate. Some children do not go home to "cheerleaders," so you need to be their cheerleaders! You need to recognize that all children can write, and therefore, you must help all children become better readers and writers. You need to "ooh" and "ahh" over each child's first attempts at writing and any subsequent improvements. In kindergarten, celebrate what each child can do, especially what they can do when they write.

Daily writing in a "journal" or writing notebook provides you with samples to share with parents. These writing samples are collected throughout the year, and they are the best way to assess reading, writing, and even "phonics" growth. Some parents may need to be reassured that their child will learn to edit and begin to work on the spelling of high-frequency words in first grade. In kindergarten, as long as you see growth and improvement, parents need not worry. Point out the children's growth by sharing these samples. ("Look, he was spelling 'like' as 'l-i-k' just last month. Now he knows there is a silent 'e' on the end of the word!")

If teachers ask kindergarten children to write only the words they know how to spell correctly, the teachers will not see the same growth in their children's writing and spelling skills. We have noticed that when teachers constantly talk about children's mistakes, some children soon stop taking risks and limit what they write to words they know. For five-year-olds, this can be very limiting! Children need to "sound" spell and use what they know about phonics to write words. This temporary spelling strategy helps children learn about letters, sounds, and words, and helps them to grow as writers.

Assessment

The best assessment of what a kindergarten student knows about reading, writing, and letter sounds is to read their daily journal writing. Are they writing more as time goes on? Is their writing getting easier to read without their help? Are their spellings becoming more conventional? You can assess, on the spot, each student's letter/sound knowledge and application (Do they use what they know?). You will also know what sounds to review or stress when working with words during the morning message, or after the Shared Reading of big books.

Celebrating Students' Writing—Young Author's Tea

The focus of a good writing program in kindergarten is on children as authors. Setting aside time for students to share their stories is an important part of the writing process. It also gives students the opportunity to develop their listening and speaking skills. After daily writing, children get to share their stories by reading (or telling) them to their classmates. Early in the year the children are asked to "circle up," hold their "driting" for everyone in the class to see, and then several children tell what they have written. Later, when writing becomes a daily occurrence, the teacher lets two to five children share their writing, using an "author's chair" format at the end of each lesson.

The last month of school is a good time for students to share with their families what they can and do write at school. If your students have been writing in journals, notebooks, or saving their stories on computer discs, you already have the stories. Now, the children simply have to "read" through their stories to decide which ones they want to publish. The word "publish" comes from the word "public," therefore, to publish is to make public! In kindergarten, we do not recommend editing these stories, as we think should be done at all grade levels above kindergarten. Kindergarten children can usually read what they have written, especially if they wrote the letters for the sounds they heard. When teachers correct their students' sound spelling, the students cannot sound it out and read it to the class.

Children need to choose "pieces" with five or more sentences. Let the children use the computer or old typewriters to "print" their stories, writing one sentence on each line. Many parents volunteer to cut 8" x 10" pieces of copy paper in half for the pages of the books. Heavier, colored construction or index paper is used for the front and back covers. The parts of the book are then stapled together, or a binding machine is used. With the help of the teacher, the teaching assistant, or some parents, the children cut out each one of their sentences. Next, they paste the title on the title page and one sentence on each of the pages. The children then illustrate each page of their books, as well as drawing a picture on the cover. In the back of each book, the teacher writes a page "About the Author," as each child dictates the information to her. As the children finish "publishing" their books, they need to return to the writing process and write some more. The children will also need to practice for the big day when they will read to their parents and other children's parents. Let them have an opportunity to do this. Set them up for success and they will be able to do their best.

Some kindergarten teachers have punch and cookies for a "Young Author's Tea" right before Mother's Day, as a present to the mothers of the children in the class. Sometimes, mothers and fathers are amazed to see so many five- and six-year-olds writing and reading! Some of these parents never wrote in kindergarten!

Alex and me will be on the same te-bol tem.

Alex and me will be on the same T-ball team.

It will be fun to run the basis.

It will be fun to run the bases.

I like to hit the ball. I like to slid. You ned to slid so you can stop.

I like to hit the ball. I like to slide. You need to slide so you can stop.

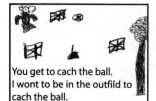

You get to cach the ball. I wont to be in the outfild to cach the ball.

You get to catch the ball. I want to be in the outfield to catch the ball.

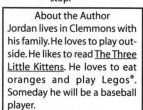

Sumday I will be on a rel baseball tem. I wont to be on the Bravs.

Some day I will be on a real baseball team. I want to be on the Braves.

About the Author
Jordan lives in Clemmons with his family. He loves to play outside. He likes to read The Three Little Kittens. He loves to eat oranges and play Legos®. Someday he will be a baseball player.

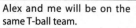

I saw a bone rabat in the wods.

I saw a brown rabbit in the woods.

He das not hav flope ers.

He does not have floppy ears.

He was the colr of stiks.

He was the color of sticks.

He luct kut. I loved ham.

He looked cute. I loved him.

He wos behind a bosh in the wods.

He was behind a bush in the woods.

Waw!! He was budfol!!!

Wow!! He was beautiful!!!

About the Author
Ashlyn loves to play in centers. She loves to write and draw! She likes to read Brown Bear, Brown Bear. She loves to eat macaroni and cheese. Someday she will be a farmer.

The Writing Center – Copying

Young students want to learn how to read, write, and spell some "interesting-to-them" words. Copying names from a predictable chart, random letters from the alphabet, or words from a poster in the writing center is often the first stage of independent writing. A picture dictionary gives teachers an organized way to provide some of those words. This easy-to-make book becomes a multilevel source because it not only supports those students who look at the words and simply copy them, it also supports those students who can read the words and are ready to learn to spell them. Teachers often put pictures that are representative of the current month or theme on a board or chart in the writing center. They fold three to five pieces of paper in half and staple them together, often with a piece of colored construction paper for a front and back cover. Each time a student visits the Writing Center, he finds his book, copies a word, and draws a picture for each of the pages. The children use pencils, pens, markers, crayons, or colored pencils to write the words. Then, they illustrate each word they write. By the end of the month, all students will have completed their books. The students can then take their picture dictionaries home and "read" the words to their families and friends.

We have created for Carson-Dellosa Publishing a package called *Building Blocks "Plus" for Kindergarten* (CD-2505) for this purpose. This set contains nine charts of pictures and words for a classroom picture dictionary. There is also an eight-page resource guide containing valuable tips and instructions for using these charts, a Morning Message chart, two cut-apart Environmental Print headers, a Getting to Know You chart, five cut-apart predictable chart headers, and a Be A Sentence Builder chart.

Creating a picture dictionary helps students to add words to their speaking, reading, and writing vocabularies. Students also learn something about letters and sounds by printing words, and they are motivated to learn to read and write some more words that are interesting to them.

The Writing Center – Writing for "Real" Reasons

The Writing Center is a place where students can practice writing for real reasons. Besides copying words from monthly theme boards or the *Building Blocks Plus* monthly charts, children are allowed to write with a variety of materials (pencils, pens, markers, and crayons), on a variety of papers (construction, newsprint, lined, half-lined, and unlined), for a variety of real reasons. During the first month of school, the children are encouraged to copy students' names, color words, and number words. Children who have written at home will have no problem with this. Some children may feel they need permission to scribble or write as best they can. They get this permission when they see the teacher model different writing styles in the first writing lessons, or when she praises and displays the work of students making their first attempts at writing.

February is a good month for writing letters and sending mail. Most kindergarten students enjoy writing pretend letters, so let your parents know that any old writing paper, notepaper, or envelopes would be appreciated. In February, a post office will fit nicely into your activities. Fill your post office with signs, stickers for stamps, envelopes, paper, rubber stamps, and a stamp pad. You may also have to borrow some money from the Math Center so that you will be in business. Children could make and mail their valentines, address envelopes, buy stamps (heart stickers), and deliver the mail on Valentine's Day. After the post office has served its purpose, a dentist's office could open in its place. For this center you will need charts, appointment cards, and an appointment book, which will give your students more reasons to write.

March is a good month for a doctor's office or health clinic. This center needs an appointment book (recycled from the dentist's office?), pencils, paper, note pads, play money, insurance forms, file folders, clipboards, an eye chart, a doctor's bag, stethoscope, etc. Children could pretend to be patients, doctors, nurses, or receptionists. Children have fun at a doctor's office or health clinic center as they read and write for real reasons.

April is a good month for a travel agency center to "plan" spring travels. If your students don't go anywhere for spring or Easter break, let them plan trips for all the places they want their kites to travel. What do teachers put in the travel agency? Some items to include are travel posters (Travel agencies sometimes give these to teachers because they do not use the same posters year after year!), a calendar, computer, paper, pencils, markers, travel brochures, etc. Some students may be able to use the computer to locate places they want to visit, while others may even know how to look up airline schedules if their parents have shown them how to do this at home!

May brings work with environmental print from cereals and restaurants. This gives teachers the opportunity for two more good center possibilities—grocery stores and restaurants. Most children know how to write menus, signs, and order tickets for their favorite fast food restaurants. If some students do not know how to do these activities, other children will be glad to share their knowledge of just what the customers and the workers do at these familiar places. You need some children to be customers who will read the menu, place their orders, and pay for their food. Other students will need to be the waiters or waitresses who write the orders or pretend to write the orders. You will also need some students to read the orders and prepare, or "cook," the food.

If you set up a grocery store, you can fill the shelves with products the children can "really read." You will need a cash register with a "scanner" (you can pretend if you don't have one) and a cashier. If you have an adding machine, you can list the prices on your products, have the cashier add up these prices, and give the customer a "receipt" with the added numbers and the total. Just like the real world, this center involves some math, reading, and writing for these kindergarten students to enjoy.

How Children Writing By Themselves Is Multilevel

Children writing by themselves is a multilevel activity if teachers let the children choose what they want to write about, and let them take as long as they need to write each "piece." It is also important for teachers to accept whatever kindergarten students can write on the first draft without demanding that they write as older writers would. Some children go through the writing/spelling stages quickly and become young authors in no time. A few children in your class will fill up a page in one sitting, and the writing they produce will exceed all expectations for five-year-olds! These children write "on their own level," far above kindergarten standards.

Other children will need more time to produce a page. These children have to sound out words and write short "pieces." They are also growing daily, but at their own speeds which are more in line with the normal growth and development of five-year-olds. Still other children struggle with this complex process. They are at the emergent stages and copy, scribble, draw, and sound out a few words using only beginning sounds and letters, but they also show progress. Their progress is simply not as fast as the progress of other students in the class. Remember that all children are different, and that cognitive growth, as well as physical growth, is slower for some children than for others. What we look for is constant growth, whether it is rapid or slow. Some children need more time to think about this complex process. With daily writing, these children will improve and that is all teachers can ask of these young writers. When teachers give children the time they need and the opportunity to write daily, they can see that writing really is a multilevel activity!

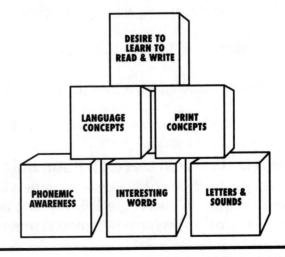

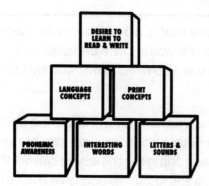

Chapter 8
Phonemic Awareness

Phonemic awareness is **not** knowing which letter makes which sound. That is phonics! Phonemic awareness is the awareness that words are composed of sounds, and is an important precursor to learning to read (Yopp, 1992). One of the best ways to help children develop the ability to manipulate sounds is through the use of children's literature that focuses on some kind of play with the sounds of language (Griffith & Olson, 1992).

An article written by Michael F. Optiz, "Children's Books to Develop Phonemic Awareness—for You and Parents, Too!" appeared in *The Reading Teacher* (Vol. 51, No. 6). This article lists children's books written in 1996 and 1997 that develop phonemic awareness. It includes ideas for using the books to develop enjoyment and phonemic awareness for both teachers and parents. The article also contains a parent's phonemic awareness observation record, which teachers could use as well.

Since phonemic awareness is also the best predictor of success in reading, teachers wonder how many children develop this important skill before they come to school. According to Adams (1991) and Cunningham & Allington (1995, 2000), only 40 to 50 percent of children come to school with sufficient phonemic awareness. Phonemic awareness is the oral before the written. Children who have phonemic awareness know:

- when words start alike (McDonald's® starts like Mommy and Michelle)

- when words rhyme (Jill and hill; hop and pop; Sam, am, and ham)

- when words are big words (hippopotamus) or small words (dog)

- if words have "lots of letters" (not the exact number) or just a few

- how to segment letter sounds (c-a-t, M-ike)

- how to play with words ("Mandy's handy dandy")

How Do Children Develop Phonemic Awareness?

Children who develop phonemic awareness before they come to school have had someone read to them, especially rhyming books and alphabet books. Someone encouraged their beginning attempts at writing and played "silly" rhyming and word games with them. ("Mad Chad was bad; now he's sad!") Children who have phonemic awareness before they come to school also know some letter names, can track print, and know some meaningful words, like their own names, Daddy, Taco Bell®, and cat.

Phonemic awareness develops through a series of stages during which children first become aware that language is made up of individual words, that words are made up of syllables, and that syllables are made up of sounds or phonemes. It is important to note here that it is not the "jargon" children learn. Five-year-olds cannot tell you how many syllables are in "beautiful," but they can clap the sounds, "beau" (clap), "ti" (clap), "ful" (clap). Likewise, they may not be able to tell you the first phoneme in Mike is the letter "M," but they can tell you that if you take the "m" sound off Mike, you would have "ike."

Children develop this phonemic awareness as a result of the oral and written language to which they are exposed. Nursery rhymes, traditional songs, chants, and *Dr. Seuss* books usually play a large role in this development. Nursery rhymes have been a part of our oral heritage for generations. We never knew how much they contributed to phonemic awareness and the ability of children to learn phonics until ten years ago. Many teachers (and politicians) still do not understand the importance of phonemic awareness before teaching phonics. For more information on phonemic awareness, see the reproducible newsletter to parents in the back of this book (pgs. 159-160). It was written by a young teacher who wanted to share her knowledge with her students' parents.

Nursery Rhymes

One of the best indicators of how well children will learn to read is their ability to recite nursery rhymes when they walk into kindergarten. The ability to recite nursery rhymes is considered an indicator of phonemic awareness. It is now known that nursery rhymes should play a large role in any kindergarten curriculum. Children need to learn to recite nursery rhymes, sing rhymes and traditional songs, clap the rhymes, and pantomime the rhymes (See Chapter 3). In some kindergarten classrooms, the teacher and her students develop "raps" for the rhymes. Once the children can recite the nursery rhymes, then the nursery rhymes can be used to teach the concept of rhyme. It is hard to give a definition of a rhyme, but children who know the nursery rhymes can tell you when words rhyme. Divide the class into halves. One half of the class says the nursery rhyme, but stops when they get to the rhyming word. The other half of the class waits to shout the rhyming word at the appropriate moment. For more information, see page 14 in *Month-by-Month Reading and Writing for Kindergarten* (CD-2401) by Dorothy Hall & Patricia Cunningham (Carson-Dellosa, 1997).

Rhyming Books – Finding Rhyming Words

Reading rhyming books develops phonemic awareness. Random House's *Dr. Seuss* books are written in rhyme. Often, as we read these books to children, they begin to guess the next rhyming word because they have paid close attention to both the pictures and the print. *Hop on Pop* by Dr. Seuss (Random House, 1963) is one such book. Children look at the pictures and the print and know it says, "hop on pop," "cup on pup," and "mouse on house." They also have to laugh when they see and hear "house on mouse" because they know a mouse could not hold up a house! Read rhyming books to your students. After you have read a rhyming book once, reread it page by page, or read two pages at a time. See if your students can find the rhyming words. Read one rhyming word, but stop just before the other in the pair. See if your students can tell you the other rhyming word. You can do this with *Zoo-Looking* by Mem Fox (Mondo Publishing, 1996). The rhyming words in this book have just one pattern, the "ack" pattern. In Chapter 3, we rounded up rhyming words with *Golden Bear* after the Shared Reading of the big book. The rhyming pairs we found in this book were all different (chair/stair, rug/bug, ice/twice, etc).

To Market, To Market by Anne Miranda (Scholastic, 1997) uses a familiar rhyme written in book form that you could also use for this activity. First, read the book to the children. Next, reread two pages at a time, stopping to ask for the rhyming words they heard. The children will tell you pig/jig, goose/loose, trout/out, lamb/swam, cow/now, duck/luck, goat/coat, disgrace/place, bed/head, too/shoe/zoo/do. It is a good idea to end right there. The last few pages of the book are just for the end of the story and do not follow the rhyme! There are lots of books in your classroom library, the media center at school, public libraries, bookstores, and on the Internet for kindergarten teachers to use to find rhyming words. Some of our favorite rhyming books are listed in Chapter 2.

Beginning Sounds or Words That Start Alike

Children who have phonemic awareness can also tell you when words start alike. Teachers can work on getting children to hear beginning sounds when working with words during the opening, tongue twisters, the morning message, and Shared Reading. Teachers can ask questions and lead children to see these relationships.

Opening

During the opening, the teacher may hold up the word card for the day of the week and ask:

- How do you know this word is 'Wednesday'?

- Can you find the word 'Wednesday' on the calendar?

- What do you notice about the word 'Wednesday'?

The answers depend upon which child you ask. Some answers include:

> "It starts with a 'W'."

> "The word 'day' is in it."

> "The word 'Wednesday' starts like 'Wal-mart™'."

> "It has more letters than the other days of the week."

The teacher then asks:

- Whose name starts like 'Wednesday'? (William, Wendy, etc.)

- Do you know any other words that begin like 'Wednesday'?

The children begin to make a list of words that begin with the "w" sound: walk, watermelon, wall, walnut, watch, etc.

Alphabet Books

Kindergarten teachers need to read alphabet books to their students. Alphabet books help children hear that certain words start with certain sounds. Over and over again, they hear that "b" is for boots in one alphabet book, ball in another alphabet book, boat in another one, and balloon in still another book. Soon the children recognize that the pictures and the words on the page begin with the same sound that the letter on the page makes at the beginning of the words. The brain is a pattern detector, and when young children first detect this pattern, they expect the pattern will hold true in other words. Reading alphabet books helps kindergarten children develop this ability. Because alphabet books help develop phonemic awareness, there are now many alphabet books available at bookstores and through catalogues for teachers and parents to purchase. Some of our favorites are listed in Chapter 2 under the "Alphabet Books" section. There are also many new alphabet books on Michael Opitz's list, contained in the article mentioned at the beginning of this chapter.

Morning Message

The morning message (See Chapter 5) develops phonemic awareness as children hear words that begin alike: morning, message, Monday, and music. The teacher helps children see this relationship by asking,

"Can anyone hear two words that begin alike in the morning message?"

"Can anyone find another word in the room that begins like these two words?"

Young students also learn the jargon of school (sentence, word, letter) by counting these elements in the morning message after it is completed.

Tongue Twisters

Tongue twisters help develop phonemic awareness. Teachers often share a "tongue twister" with the class during the "opening," or while children are in "big group." As children listen to the teacher say the tongue twister, they hear the same sound at the beginning of most of the words. Once they hear that the beginning sounds are alike, they are ready to see that the same letter is at the beginning of those words. Next, ask if anyone else has a name that begins with that sound. If you make the list on the board, the class can see if those names all begin with the same letter, too. The final question should be whether they know any other words that begin with that sound and letter. Tongue twisters help link phonemic awareness (oral) and phonics (written or visual). See page 59 in *Month-by-Month Reading and Writing for Kindergarten* (CD-2401) for a list of tongue twisters you can use. An even better idea is to create tongue twisters with your student's names in them. One teacher on the teachers.net mailring listed some of the tongue twisters her class came up with:

Lovely Laura likes licorice and lollipops.

Can Carl cook corn, cabbage, and cake?

Merry Mary makes meatballs and macaroni.

John jumps over James, Jennifer, and Justin.

Clapping Syllables and Hearing Sounds

Another activity that may help children listen to words and separate the words into the sounds or the beats they hear is "clapping syllables." You can do this with the children's names. Tell the children you are going to say the names of several children in the class and they are to listen for the beats they hear. Ask the children to clap the number of beats each name has. Say each name one at a time. Help the children, as needed, to decide that Hannah is a two-beat name and has two claps, John is a one-beat name and has one clap, Sally is a two-beat and has two claps, Eleanor is a three-beat name and has three claps, etc. Once the children can do this by hearing the names, begin to have them look at the names as they clap the beats. Explain that if a name has more claps, it probably takes more letters to write. "How many claps does Angelica have? Chad? Mandy?"

Playing Silly Games with Words

Have you listened to young children on the playground when they want to tease each other? What do they say? Often, you hear chants such as "Fat Pat ate a rat!" "Bad Chad is sad!" or "Silly Billy is chilly!" The children are becoming aware of words and sounds and can manipulate these to express themselves and to impress others! Some children name their toys with rhyming pairs like "Claire Bear" or "Gayle the Whale." Children and rhymes just seem to go together. Children love to chant, sing, and make up raps and rhymes.

Most kindergarten teachers have an amazing store of rhymes and fingerplays to go with their units or themes throughout the year. They can use *One, Two, Buckle My Shoe* when they are teaching children to count, *Five Little Pumpkins* for October, *A Turkey Sat on a Backyard Fence* for Thanksgiving, and *The Itsy, Bitsy Spider* when studying weather. Some kindergarten teachers seem to have a knack for remembering a rhyme or fingerplay for just about everything they want to do in school.

Some books we like on this topic are:

Phonemic Awareness: Playing with Sounds to Strengthen Beginning Reading Skills by Jo Fitzpatrick (Creative Teaching Press, 1997)

Fall Phonemic Awareness: Songs and Rhymes by Jo Kimberly Jordano and Trisha Callella-Jones (Creative Teaching Press, 1998)

Winter Phonemic Awareness: Songs and Rhymes by Jo Kimberly Jordano and Trisha Callella-Jones (Creative Teaching Press, 1998)

Spring Phonemic Awareness: Songs and Rhymes by Jo Kimberly Jordano and Trisha Callella-Jones (Creative Teaching Press, 1998)

Phonemic awareness is an important precursor for learning to read. When kindergarten teachers work on phonemic awareness, the other blocks are also strengthened.

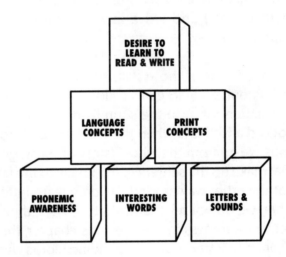

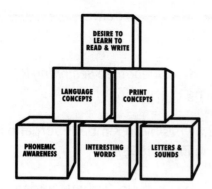

Chapter 9
Phonics...or
Letters and Sounds

Teaching phonics has long been a part of teaching reading in the primary grades in this country. Years ago, kindergarten was thought to be a place to socialize and for children to learn how to get along before formal learning began in first grade. Along with our country's zeal to be the best and have the best came the pressure for children to do everything sooner and better without regard to what was developmentally appropriate for young students. Thus, the teaching of reading was pushed into kindergarten with very few adaptations. Not that some children are not ready to learn to read, but some practices are not multilevel and therefore are "boring" for some children and "stressful" for other children. We now know that children can learn to read and write in kindergarten if it is done in a developmentally appropriate way.

Phonics is one of those skills that all children can learn if it is not a memorization task. Phonics is learned as children have meaningful encounters with reading and as children listen to the sounds in words. Next, the letters and letter sounds are noticed and this is when the teacher needs to introduce letters and letter names. Thus, we go from the whole (story or message) to the sentence, then to the words that make up the sentence, and finally to the letters and the sounds they make, and not the other way around. Children learn letters and sounds so much more easily when we do not tell them what we want them to learn. Having talked about phonemic awareness in the previous chapter, this chapter discusses the teaching of phonics or letter sounds in Building Blocks classrooms.

Beginning Letters/Sounds

Children who have phonemic awareness can tell you when words start alike. They soon learn that letters have sounds and that these sounds sound something like the letter names! During the opening, teachers can help children focus on hearing beginning sounds when talking about familiar words (days, specials, and weather words). The class can focus on words that begin alike during tongue twisters, the morning message, and the Shared Reading of big books. Once children can hear that some words begin alike, then the teacher is ready to call attention to the print and have the children look at the letters making those sounds at the beginning of words. We do not teach letters and sounds with work sheets and workbooks in Building Blocks classrooms. We believe phonics can be taught the same way children who come to school reading have learned phonics, by using letters and sounds during real reading and writing activities. Teachers can ask questions and lead children to see these relationships while doing the activities we have discussed in the previous eight chapters.

The Opening

During the opening, the teacher may hold up the word card for the day of the week and ask:

- How do you know this word is Monday?

- Can you find the word Monday on the calendar?

- What do you notice about the word Monday?

The questions call attention to the print on the word card the teacher is holding, or has placed in a pocket chart. The answers will depend upon which child she asks. Some answers include:

"It starts with an 'M.'"

"The word 'day' is in it."

"Monday starts like Mommy."

"Monday has six letters in it."

Notice that all the answers are about the print, but they are all different. Different children are at different places in their learning, and when you ask, "What letter does this begin with?" or "What sound does this letter make?" you are asking a "grade level" question, not a multilevel question where there is something for everyone.

The teacher next asks:

- Whose name starts like Monday? (Mandy, Matthew, and Mary.)

- Do you know any other words that begin like Monday?

Once again, the answers to these questions will depend on the children in your class. On the board, the teacher begins a list of words that begin with the "m" sound, writing as the children call them out to her: mother, muffins, moose, milk, macaroni, map, money, magic, etc.

Alphabet Books

Kindergarten teachers need to read alphabet books to their students. Alphabet books help children hear that certain words start with certain sounds. Kindergarten classes can make a class alphabet book from a predictable chart using the letter names: "A is for___. B is for _____. C is for _____ , etc. (See page 63 in CD-2401, *Month-by-Month Reading and Writing for Kindergarten*.) We like to make a class book titled *ABC and You* using the children's names. This activity is patterned after the big book *ABC and You* by Eugenie Fernandes (Houghton Mifflin Co., 1985). Put the letter "A" on the chart first and then ask the students whose names begin with A to stand up. Write each name beside the letter it starts with, and for each child, include a descriptive adjective that begins with the same letter. If there isn't a student in your class for every letter, leave the letter blank or make up a name and adjective. This is an example of how the chart begins:

ABC and YOU

A . . . Adorable Angelica

B . . .

C . . . Cheerful Chad

. . . Colorful Corey

. . . Cute Chris

D . . . Daring David

Later in the year, some kindergarten teachers have the children make their own individual alphabet books. They fold 13 or 14 pieces of plain white paper in half, and staple the book together with a front and back cover. On each page, they have the children write a capital and small letter, and then draw a picture of something that begins with that letter. Some teachers have the students find pictures at home for homework and bring in a picture for a certain letter of the alphabet. (Before you ask your students to do this, think, "Do most of my students have magazines at home?") Children can do this in school if they do not have magazines at home. Some teachers send magazines and blunt-edged scissors home with the students who do not have them. The children cut and paste a picture or pictures from magazines and/or catalogues on the correct pages. Some children can even write the words to go with the pictures.

Another idea for a class alphabet book is to do animal alphabet books; this works especially well if the class is doing a theme on animals. You can also make classroom alphabet books, using student pictures of objects in the classroom that begin with the different letters of the alphabet (alphabet, board, colors, door, eraser, etc.). Making alphabet books, including class alphabet big books and individual alphabet books, helps kindergarten students see the relationships between letters and sounds.

Morning Message
The morning message (See Chapter 5) helps develop phonemic awareness as children hear words that begin alike: morning, message, Monday, and music. It also helps children learn letters and sounds (phonics) as they discover that the words which sound alike usually begin with the same letter.

The teacher helps children see this relationship by asking,

"Can anyone hear two words that begin alike in the morning message?"

"Can anyone find another word in the room that begins like these two words?"

Young students also learn the jargon of school (sentence, word, letter, beginning sounds, etc.,) by counting the sentences, words and letters in the morning message. They also notice that some sounds are made up of more than one letter!

Often the teacher makes sure that certain words appear in the morning message. During the week of the county fair she might write:

We had fun at the fair. We saw five fish and a farmer.

After the teacher finishes the message she asks,

"Does anyone see any words that begin like 'fair'?"

"Does anyone know any other words that start like 'fair'?"

Once again the lesson began with the whole (the morning message about the fair), then the teacher stopped and looked at the sentences and asked some questions about those sentences, and ended with a phonics lesson about the "f" letter and sound.

Tongue Twisters

Tongue twisters help develop phonemic awareness and help with the transition to phonics, starting with the oral and then going to the written. As children listen to the teacher say the tongue twisters, they hear the same sounds at the beginning of most of the words. Once they hear that the beginning sounds are alike, they are ready to see that the same letters are at the beginning of those words. If the teacher has written the tongue twister on a chart, or placed a sentence strip in a pocket chart for the children to see, then everyone is ready for the next step. The teacher has the students look at the beginning of the words where they hear the same sounds to see if the same letter is at the beginning of the words. Next, the teacher asks if anyone has a name that begins with that letter and sound. She writes those names on the board near the tongue twister for everyone to see that they begin with the same letter, too. Finally, she asks the question, "Do you know any other words that begin with that sound and letter?" Then, she writes the students' words on the board so that the whole class can see that they begin with the same letter and sound, too. Tongue twisters help link phonemic awareness (oral) and phonics (written or visual) by starting with a sentence (the whole), moving to words (parts), and then to letters (smaller parts). You can make tongue twisters even more meaningful by making up your own using your students' names, and then posting them on a chart or the board where you can refer to them all week.

Writing with "Phonics" Spelling

As we have said before, to really understand what your students know about phonics, look at their daily writing (Chapter 7). When children use scribbles and random letters they have not grasped the concept that certain letters make certain sounds. That is why the stage is called prephonemic (i.e., before they understand about phonemes, or letter sounds).

When kindergarten students first understand this letter/sound relationship, they represent whole words with the letters they hear at the beginning of the words. We have noticed that in kindergarten classrooms using Building Blocks strategies, the children go through this stage quite quickly. Teachers who are observant will notice this stage in their struggling students. These students work hard to represent the sounds they are learning with the letters the teacher is talking about each day. The children stretch out the word, but only write one letter, usually the beginning letter, unless it is a vowel. Sometimes kindergarten children stretch out a long word and write the beginning and ending letter as if there was nothing in the middle! When children use "invented" spelling or "sound" spelling, their writing is very phonetic. The letters they write are exactly what they hear. These young students soon see some words over and over again and learn these high frequency words (is, come, like, have). They begin to realize that words aren't always spelled like they sound, at least not in English! When they learn words like "at" and see that spelling pattern in "cat," "hat," "fat," "mat," and "Pat," they learn that certain groups of letters or patterns make certain sounds.

Making Words

Making Words (Cunningham and Hall, 1994, 1997; Cunningham & Cunningham, 1994)) in most elementary classrooms is a multilevel phonics and spelling activity in which the students are given a certain number of letter cards and are asked to manipulate these letters to make some words. In kindergarten, we do not use the individual letter cards because some children are not ready for this activity. We do make words, but in a different format that is more appropriate for younger students.

When Building Blocks teachers work with rhyming words and rhyming patterns (-ack, -at, -ill, -un, etc.) after reading a rhyme or rhyming book, like *The Cat in the Hat* by Dr. Seuss (Random House, 1957), they might do a making words lesson. The teacher could use teacher-made yarned necklaces or child-sized letter vests instead of the small letter cards. The teacher has the children become the letters while they wear these yarned necklaces or vests and "make words."

She talks about the pattern (-at) and has the two children wearing those letters ("a" and "t") come to the front of the class. Next, she has other children "join" them, wearing the letters "b," "h," "c," "f," "p," "r," "s," and "m." She may describe names and how if the word "pat" were a name, then it would have to be a capital letter. The teacher may also have two children come up together and make the words brat, flat, chat, scat, and that.

There is a system and a pattern in the way letters represent sounds. Our instruction should point out these patterns. Children who see new words and ask themselves how those words are like other words they know can discover many patterns on their own.

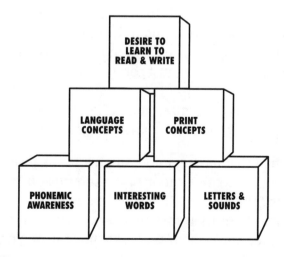

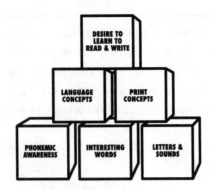

Chapter 10
Interesting Words

There are two kinds of learning based on the brain's two types of memory stores. Tasks we just do "over and over again" until we learn them are put in our rote memory store. This rote memory store has a limited capacity, and if we do not practice something that is contained in the rote memory store for a while then the rote memory store gives the space over to something more current. (What was her phone number? I used to know it when I called her everyday. What is his zip code? I used to know it when I had to send him a weekly report. Now I have to look it up again!) The other memory store is the associative memory store; it has an unlimited capacity. We find things in the associative memory store that we have not used for years if the memory is triggered by the right image, smell, song, etc.

Elaine Williams has a wonderful story about her memory and her "trips" all over the Carolinas and neighboring states doing workshops for kindergarten teachers. She tells of the many long drives she made when she was tired and all her tapes seemed to be putting her to sleep. To avoid nodding off, she searches her radio for a station that is playing the "oldies". Listening to the "oldies" brings back memories of people and places in the past. She says the songs have "associations" and soon her mind is awake thinking back to her high school and college days, as each song evokes another set of memories. While it is a daily chore for most of us to remember where we put our car keys or to whom we wrote our last check, those old songs, because of the associations they stimulate, bring back memories of decades long gone by!

The trick to putting information in the associative memory store rather than the rote memory store is to make an association or "connection" with the information. Children who are trying to learn that a particular shape turned a particular way is called an "m" and that "m" makes a certain sound, cannot simply remember this information. They must connect the "m" to some words that they do know that begin with the same letter and sound. When the new words they are learning begin like words they know that are "interesting to the them" (like Mommy, Michelle, Matthew, McDonald's®, etc.), it makes remembering this information an easier task.

When children put information into their rote memory store and it is not used for awhile (a week vacation or the summer off), then it is forgotten. Why does this happen? The reason is that some children don't have a way to pull the information up again from their rote memory. Thus, it is important for children to learn some "important to them" words so they can begin to make those connections. The only way to help put letter name and sound knowledge into the associative store rather than the rote store is to make sure they can read some words that make connections. Often the easiest words to learn are words that are interesting to them, like their names, Mommy and Daddy, sibling's names, friend's names, favorite restaurants, sports teams, and favorite products. When the teacher says, "M says 'mmmmmm,'" the child puts "M" into the associative store when she connects the sound to words she knows and says to herself, "Like Michelle (her name), Mommy (another important person in her life) and McDonald's® (her favorite restaurant). Because she knows how to read some words that begins with the "m" sound, Michelle is able to put the information into the associative store and can use it anytime she needs it. The child who does not know certain words has to memorize the information and hope he can remember it the next day when he is called on. He has not put the information into the brain with an association or "connection" and therefore has no way to "pull it up" when needed.

In this chapter we will work on ways to help young students learn some "interesting-to-them" words, like names, favorite restaurants, and cereals. These words will help them to make connections and to put words in the associative store when needed and to pull the words out of memory when needed to remember letters and sounds.

Names – "Getting To Know You"

Most kindergarten teachers begin the year with some get-acquainted activities. As a part of these activities, teachers often focus on a special child each day. In addition to learning about each of their classmates, students can focus attention on the special child's name and use the name to develop some important understandings about words and letters.

To prepare for this activity, you need to write all the children's first names (put an initial for the last name if two names are the same), using a permanent marker on sentence strips. Cut the strips so that the long names have long strips and short names have short strips. Place the strips in a box. Each day, reach into the box and draw out a name. This child becomes the "Special Student for the Day" and her name becomes the focus of the many activities. Reserve a bulletin board and add each child's name to the board as it is selected. Some teachers have the children bring in a snapshot of themselves or take pictures of the children to add to the board along with their names. Other teachers may have the class draw pictures of the "special child" so that they can put together a class book at the end of the activity. The teacher then titles this book "Our Class," and places it in the reading center for the students to read and enjoy. Because it contains the names of their classmates, and their classmates names are both meaningful and interesting, it is not surprising that many kindergarten children can read these books cover to cover. "Getting to Know You" is not just a way to get to know the other students, but also to learn about letter/sound relationships in a way that makes sense to young children. On the following pages are some examples of activities you might do with your students' names.

First Name, First Day

The teacher closes her eyes, reaches into the box, shuffles the names around, and then draws one name (John) out. She calls John to the front and names him "Special Student" for the day! She leads the other children in interviewing this child. She finds out what John likes to eat, games he likes to play, things he does after school, etc. Does he have a brother or sister? Cat? Dog? Gerbil? Other pet? Next, she focuses the children's attention on the special child's name, "John." She points to the word "John" on the sentence strip and helps the class understand "school jargon" by pointing out that this "word" is John's name. The teacher tells the student that this word has four "letters" in it and lets them help her count the letters. She says, "J-o-h-n" and has the children chant the letters along with her. The teacher points out that John's name begins with the **letter** "J." She explains that the "J" looks bigger than the other letters because it is a **capital** J and the other letters are **small letters** (or **uppercase** and **lowercase**, depending on the jargon you use).

Next, the teacher lets John lead the class in a cheer using the letters in his name:

> "Give me a J," (which often sounds like, "Gimme a J")
>
> "Give me an "o,"
>
> "Give me a "h,"
>
> "Give me an "n,"
>
> "What have you got?" asks John.
>
> "John," his classmates answer.
>
> "What have you got?" asks John.
>
> "John," his classmates answer.
>
> Together the teacher and class end the cheer with, "Yay!"

The teacher takes a blank sentence strip and has the students watch her write the word John. She has them chant the spelling of this name as she writes the letters. Next, she cuts the letters apart, mixes them up, and lets John arrange the letters in the right order in the pocket chart so that they spell his name.

For the next activity, the teacher gives each child (including John) a large sheet of drawing paper, and lets the students use crayons to write "John" in large letters on one side of the paper. She models at the chalkboard how to write each letter as they write it. She is not worried if what the children write is not perfect (or even bears little resemblance to what she wrote), and resists the temptation to correct what they write. She remembers that children who write at home before coming to school often reverse letters and make them in funny ways.

Finally, the teacher has everyone look at John and describe him. "John has one head, two eyes, one nose, one mouth, two ears, a neck, a body, two arms, two legs, and two feet." She talks about his clothes, "John is wearing a blue shirt, blue jeans, and white shoes with black stripes. Then, she lets the children draw a picture of John on their drawing paper. The teacher saves the drawing John did of himself with his name on it and posts it on the "Special Student" bulletin board. She lets John take the other students' drawings of him home!

The important concept for students to understand is that names are words, that words can be written and that it takes a few letters to write some words and lots of letters to write other words.

Second Name, Second Day
The teacher closes her eyes, reaches into the box, shuffles the names around, and then draws one out. She calls Hannah forward and names her "Special Student" for the day! The teacher leads the other children in interviewing Hannah. (Remember what you did for the first child because every child that follows will expect the same treatment.) Next, the teacher focuses the children's attention on Hannah's name. She points to the word Hannah, and tells the students that this name has six "letters" in it, and lets them help her count the letters. The teacher says, "H-a-n-n-a-h" and has the children chant the letters along with her. She points out that Hannah's name begins with the **letter** "H." She explains that the "H" looks bigger than the other letters because it is a **capital** "H" and the other letters are **small letters**. Then the teacher lets Hannah lead the class in a cheer using the letters in her name.

Taking a blank sentence strip, the teacher has the students watch her write the word, "Hannah." She also has them chant the spelling of this name as she writes the letters. Then, she cuts the letters apart, mixes them up, and lets Hannah arrange the letters in the right order in the pocket chart so that they spell her name. "How many letters are there in Hannah's name?" Next, the teacher compares Hannah's name to John's name. "Who has the most letters?" "Whose name has the fewest letters?" "Do they have any of the same letters?"

The teacher gives each child, including Hannah, a large sheet of drawing paper, and lets the students use crayons to write "Hannah" in large letters on one side of the paper. As they write, the teacher goes to the chalkboard and models how to write each letter. She has everyone look at Hannah and describe what she is wearing. Finally, she lets the children draw pictures of Hannah on their drawing paper. The teacher saves the drawing Hannah did of herself and posts it on the "Special Student" bulletin board. She lets Hannah take the other students' drawings of her home.

Third Name, Third Day
The teacher closes her eyes, reaches into the box, shuffles the names around, and then draws a name out. She calls Paul forward and names him "Special Student" for the day! The teacher leads the other children in interviewing Paul. Next, the teacher focuses the children's attention on Paul's name. She points to the word Paul, and tells the students that this name has four letters in it, and lets them help her count the letters. The teacher says, "P-a-u-l" and has the children chant the letters along with her. She points out that Paul's name begins with the **letter** "P." She explains that the "P" looks bigger than the other letters because it is a **capital** "P" and the other letters are **small letters.** Then the teacher lets Paul lead the class in a cheer using the letters in his name.

Taking a blank sentence strip, the teacher has the students watch her write the word, "Paul." She also has them chant the spelling of this name as she writes the letters. Then, she cuts the letters apart, mixes them up, and lets Paul arrange the letters in the right order in the pocket chart so that they spell his name. "How many letters are there in Paul's name?" Next, the teacher compares Paul's name to John's and Hannah's names. "Who has the most letters?" "Whose name has the fewest letters?" "Do they have any of the same letters?"

The teacher gives each child, including Paul, a large sheet of drawing paper, and lets the students use crayons to write "Paul" in large letters on one side of the paper. As they write, the teacher goes to the chalkboard and models how to write each letter. She has everyone look at Paul and describe what he is wearing. Finally, she lets the children draw pictures of Paul on their drawing paper. The teacher saves the drawing Paul did of himself and posts it on the "Special Student" bulletin board. She lets Paul take the other students' drawings of him home.

Fourth Name, Fourth Day

The teacher closes her eyes, reaches into the box, shuffles the names around, and then draws one out. She calls Mandy forward and names her "Special Student" for the day! The teacher leads the other children in interviewing Mandy. Next, the teacher focuses the children's attention on Mandy's name. She points to the word Mandy, and tells the students that this name has five "letters" in it, and lets them help her count the letters. The teacher says, "M-a-n-d-y" and has the children chant the letters along with her. She points out that Mandy's name begins with the **letter** "M." She explains that the "M" looks bigger than the other letters because it is a **capital** "M" and the other letters are **small letters**. Then the teacher lets Mandy lead the class in a cheer using the letters in her name.

Taking a blank sentence strip, the teacher has the students watch her write the word, "Mandy." She also has them chant the spelling of this name as she writes the letters. Then, she cuts the letters apart, mixes them up, and lets Mandy arrange the letters in the right order in the pocket chart so that they spell her name. "How many letters are there in Mandy's name?" Next, the teacher compares Mandy's name to the other names already on the bulletin board. "Who has the most letters?" "Whose name has the fewest letters?" "Do they have any of the same letters?"

The teacher gives each child, including Mandy, a large sheet of drawing paper, and lets the students use crayons to write "Mandy" in large letters on one side of the paper. As they write, the teacher goes to the chalkboard and models how to write each letter. She has everyone look at Mandy and describe what she is wearing. Finally, she lets the children draw pictures of Mandy on their drawing paper. The teacher saves the drawing Mandy did of herself and posts it on the "Special Student" bulletin board. She lets Mandy take the other students' drawings of her home.

Fifth Name, Fifth Day

Again, the teacher closes her eyes, reaches into the box, shuffles the names around, and then draws one out. She calls Angelica forward and names her "Special Student" for the day! The teacher leads the other children in interviewing Angelica. Next, the teacher focuses the children's attention on Angelica's name. She points to the word Angelica, and tells the students that this name has five "letters" in it, and lets them help her count the letters. The teacher says, "A-n-g-e-l-i-c-a" and has the children chant the letters along with her. She points out that Mandy's name begins with the **letter** "A." She explains that the "A" looks bigger than the other letters because it is a **capital** "A" and the other letters are **small letters**. Then the teacher lets Angelica lead the class in a cheer using the letters in her name.

Taking a blank sentence strip, the teacher has the students watch her write the word, "Angelica." She also has them chant the spelling of this name as she writes the letters. Then, she cuts the letters apart, mixes them up, and lets Angelica arrange the letters in the right order in the pocket chart so that they spell her name. "How many letters are there in Angelica's name?" Next, the teacher compares Angelica's name to the four names that are already on the bulletin board. "Whose name has the most letters?" "Whose name has the fewest letters?" "Do they have any of the same letters?"

The teacher gives each child, including Angelica, a large sheet of drawing paper, and lets the students use crayons to write "Angelica" in large letters on one side of the paper. As they write, the teacher goes to the chalkboard and models how to write each letter. She has everyone look at Angelica and describe what she is wearing. Finally, she lets the children draw pictures of Angelica on their drawing paper. The teacher saves the drawing Angelica did of herself and posts it on the "Special Student" bulletin board. She lets Angelica take the other students' drawings of her home.

The fascinating thing about this activity is how the children compare their own names to the ones on the board even before their names are chosen. This is exactly the kind of word/letter awareness you are trying to develop!

If all the student's names are on the "Special Student" Bulletin Board or a "Names" Word Wall (putting student's names on a Word Wall would be an appropriate use of a Word Wall in kindergarten!), you can now use these names as associative links to letters and sounds. The next time around choosing the "Special Student" the teacher can point out these associations if the children don't see them.

Imagine that the names of the children displayed on the bulletin board are:

Steve	Patty	Janet	Mandy	Tracy
Corey	Julie	Chris	John	José
Mary	Angelica	Hannah	David	Chad
Shawn	Susan	Sally	Eleanor	Julio
Kristen	Karen	Matthew	Jamarcio	

Mary is chosen as the first "Special Student" the second time around. The teacher has all the students with an "m" in their names come to the bulletin board (Word Wall) and point to the "m." There are four "m's" in all. There are three names with an "m" at the beginning (Mary, Mandy, and Matthew) and one name with an "m" in the middle (Jamarcio). The teacher says each name, stretching it out. She asks the class to decide if they can hear the usual sound of the letter. For "m," the class says that they can hear the usual sound in all of these names.

On the next day, Julie is chosen, so all the students who have a "j" in their names go to the board and point to their names. The teacher asks the students to count the number of times they see the letter "j" on the board. (Janet, Julie, John, José, and Julio = 5 times)

> "Do you find those j's at the beginning, middle, or end of the names? That's right! They are at the beginning. Stretch out those names and decide if you hear the same sound at the beginning of those names. Three of the names have the usual sound—Janet, John, and Julie. Two of the names have a different sound. The j's at the beginning of Julio and José have 'h' sounds."

The teacher and her class continue doing this with all the students' names. Chad is next, so the teacher asks them questions about "c."

> "How many names have a 'c'?." How many have a 'c' at the beginning of their name? Do they sound alike? Which ones have the usual sound at the beginning? What sound do you hear at the beginning of Chad and Chris? What letters make those sounds? How many c's do you see or hear somewhere in the middle? Stretch those names out and listen for the sound 'c' makes. Is it the usual sound?"

Children will learn a lot about letters and sounds by comparing the letters and sounds in the names of the students in their class. Having the names posted in the room gives the children an opportunity to do this anytime they come to a new word.

How "Getting to Know You" Is Multilevel

"Getting to Know You" is a truly multilevel activity. All of the children learn the names of their classmates, and they also learn something about each of their classmates on the day each one is "spotlighted." Some children will learn to read and write the names of their classmates, and as they focus on which names have which letter, they will learn letter names and sounds, too. Other students begin to associate letters and sounds with the names they are learning, while they are also learning print concepts and school "jargon."

Environmental Print

If children are to improve their reading and writing skills, as well as word knowledge, they must have practice. Some children see the people who live in their homes reading and writing on a daily basis. Other children do not have this exposure at home. Teachers want children to "practice" at home some of the things they do in school. One way to do this is with environmental print. Most children know their favorite cereals, drinks, and fast-food restaurants. Many children (and adults) who cannot actually read can still recognize the logo of the products they see and use on a daily basis. If you want children to practice letter names, teach them by using the cereal boxes that are found in their homes.

Cereals

Bring in several different boxes of popular cereals, or have the students bring in empty boxes from home. Talk about the different cereals and see how many students eat them for breakfast each day. Graph the class's favorite cereals and see which brands and types are the most popular.

For this activity, the teacher starts with the class's favorite brand of cereal. She holds up the box and has the children look at it, then talks about the colors and the pictures on the box. The teacher has the children count the letters in the cereal name with her. Since the class's favorite cereal is *Kellogg's Frosted Flakes*®, she counts, "1, 2, 3, 4, 5, 6, 7, 8, 9, 10, 11, 12, 13. There are 13 letters in Frosted Flakes." Then, she has the children say the letters with her, "F-r-o-s-t-e-d, space, F-l-a-k-e-s."

Next, the teacher passes out laminated letter cards. The letters should be identical to the letters on the box. She asks the children with the letter cards to come to the front of the class and stand in the right order. She points to each child holding a laminated letter and has the child say the letter name on the card. Then, she collects the letters and has the children return to their seats.

Holding the box up again, the teacher asks, "What do you notice about the box?" She hears responses like:

"Frosted Flakes is two words."

"Frosted Flakes are in a blue box."

"Frosted Flakes begins like Freida's name."

"Frosted Flakes ends with an 's.'"

After discussing the box, the brand name, and the letters, the teacher places the laminated letters in a pocket chart to form the words "Frosted Flakes." She lets the children write the words "Frosted Flakes" with blue crayons or markers and then she has them draw a picture of the box (*Tony the Tiger*™ and all). The teacher is sure to say, "That's Great!" to every child who is doing a good job! Once she has spelled out the names of several cereals, she knows that her students will be able to practice letter names each morning at the breakfast table. Young children enjoy showing off what they have learned in school and cereal boxes are found in most homes.

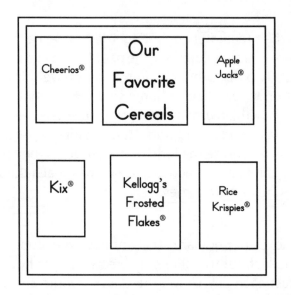 

Restaurants

It is hard to drive through any city or town without seeing restaurant signs. The bags and food wrappers that the students and their parents bring home from each restaurant advertise the restaurants' names and the products they sell. Talk about the different restaurants the students visit and see how many they can list. Bring in bags or food wrappers with these restaurant logos (names) on them. Most kindergarten children can "read" the logos of their favorite restaurants. Graph their favorites and see which restaurants are the most popular for the children in your classroom. Talk about these popular restaurants, discussing a different one each day.

For this example, Taco Bell® is the class's favorite restaurant, so the teacher starts with it. She holds up a Taco Bell bag, and has the children look at it as she talks about the colors and the pictures on it. The teacher asks, "What does the Taco Bell logo have to do with its name?" She has the children count the letters in Taco Bell with her, "1, 2, 3, 4, 5, 6, 7, 8. There are 8 letters in Taco Bell." Then she has the children say the letter names with her, "T-a-c-o, space, B-e-l-l."

Next, the teacher passes out laminated letter cards. The letters are identical to the letters on the bag. She asks the children with the letter cards to come to the front of the class and stand in the right order. The teacher points to each child holding a laminated letter and has him say the letter name on the card. Then, the teacher collects the letters and has the children return to their seats. Holding the bag up again, she asks, "What do you notice about the bag?" She may hear responses like:

"There is a picture of a bell on the bag."

"Taco Bell is two words."

"Taco begins with a 't' and Bell begins with a 'b.'"

"Both Taco and Bell begin with capital letters."

After discussing the bag, the brand name, and the letters, the teacher places the laminated letters in the pocket chart to form the words "Taco Bell." She lets the children write the words "Taco Bell" with black crayons or markers and then has them draw a picture of the Taco Bell logo.

Once you have spelled out the names of several popular restaurants, you know that children will have many opportunities to practice letter names as they drive down the main streets of your town, go out to eat, or see their parents bring home fast food. Young children enjoy showing off what they have learned in school about letters and sounds. Fast food restaurants, like cereal boxes, give children the opportunity to do this every day, even if they do not come from homes with magazines and books. Learning familiar and "interesting-to-them" words is fascinating for most kindergarten students.

Taco Bell® is being used by permission of Taco Bell Corporation.

143*The Teacher's Guide to Building Blocks*

Teams and Products

College and professional football and basketball teams, professional athletes and mascots, as well as candy and soft drink logos are more examples of environmental print, which provide opportunities for youngsters to learn to read, write, and practice letters. Don't let the year pass without doing activities like these in school. Environmental print provides children the opportunity to practice letter names all year long, and it is also something they can practice during the summer months when you are not there to help them.

Appropriate Word Walls for Kindergarten

We do not use Word Walls in our kindergarten classrooms because there is print everywhere in our rooms! The morning message, predictable charts, color words, number words, days of the week, months of the year, names, Writing Center picture dictionary words, science and social studies themes, and environmental print boards are all displayed and used. There is never a time in kindergarten when students have to recognize and spell words correctly as they do in first grade with the Word Wall. Some teachers like to put their students' names on a Word Wall, along with some high frequency words they have worked with and taught. If students are going to learn about print, it must have meaning to them and it must be part of the instructional program. Below are two pictures of Word Walls we think are appropriate for kindergarten. One is a "Names" Word Wall, and the other one is an "Environmental Print" (Products) Word Wall.

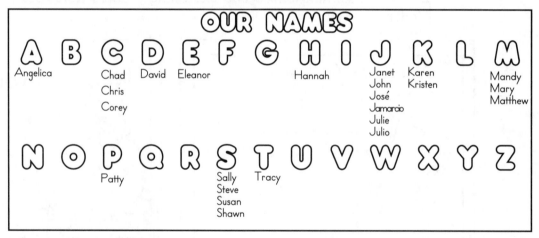

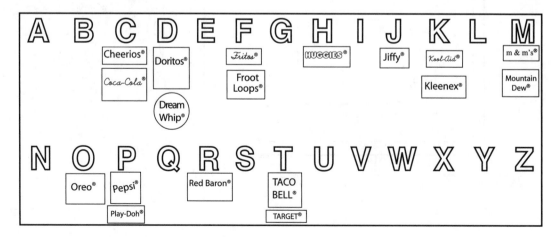

Some kindergarten programs, including many basal companies, now have words for children to "master" during kindergarten. However, you must remember that kindergarten students do not usually learn to read and write words by memorizing them. They will only learn these words if they have many meaningful encounters with them all year. They must make connections to other words they know before they are expected to "learn" them.

In a "developmentally appropriate" kindergarten class, the only Word Wall you will need during the first quarter of the school year is one with your students' names on it. If you are writing morning messages each day, writing predictable charts each week, and doing all the activities that are suggested including making class books, then your students are probably very familiar with several high frequency words already. These words may include: *is* (Today *is*___.), *can* (I *can*___.), *I* (*I* go to ____.), *we* (*We* will___.), *go* (We *go* to___.), etc. These meaningful encounters are much better for learning words than merely placing them on a word wall.

During the last quarter of the school year, many teachers put up some of these familiar, high-frequency words in their classroom. They often put them in the Writing Center or near the computer. Many times they are written on a word worm, or they are written on cut-out pieces of "popcorn," to signify that the words keep popping up in students' reading and writing.

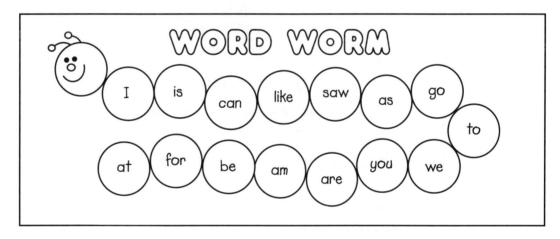

A Print-Rich Environment Is the Best Word Wall for Kindergarten!

A print-rich environment is the best "word wall" for a kindergarten class. All the print in the classroom must have meaning to the students and it must be part of the instructional program. When words are learned from frequent encounters and not just memorized, children will use them when they read and write. Otherwise, words are often forgotten over the summer and the first grade teacher says, "Didn't their kindergarten teacher teach them anything?" It is not only what we do, but how we do it that is important in teaching. Children can learn to read and write, and they can become very good at reading and writing, if it is done in a developmentally appropriate way!

Assessing Progress

In order to determine how various children are developing in their reading, writing, and word knowledge, teachers need to be keen observers of children. The most practical diagnostic tool for this purpose is Marie Clay's *An Observation Survey of Early Literacy Achievement* (Heinemann Books, 1993). This survey, first developed as a screening device for Reading Recovery, has been adapted for classroom use. It is a valid and authentic measure of children's emergent literacy behaviors. This survey may become a part of kindergarten assessment.

Many teachers have come up with their own ways of observing children's early reading and writing progress. Here are some behaviors to observe as you assess student development, as listed in *Phonics They Use: Words for Reading and Writing* by P. Cunningham (HarperCollins, 1995):

- Students read (or "pretend read") favorite books, poems, songs, and chants.

- Students write in whatever way they can, and they can read what they wrote even if no one else can.

- Students track print—they point to the words using left-right/top-bottom conventions.

- Students know critical jargon—they can point to just one word, the first word in the sentence, just one letter, the first letter in the word, the longest word, etc.

- Students recognize and can write some concrete words—their names and names of other children, days of the week, and favorite words from books, poems, and chants.

- Students demonstrate phonemic awareness; they orally manipulate words by taking off letters and changing the first letters to make words rhyme.

- Students recognize words that rhyme and can make up rhymes.

- Students can name many letters and can tell you words that begin with common initial sounds.

- Students are learning more about the world they live in and are able to talk about what they know.

- Students can listen to stories and informational books and retell the most important information. They see themselves as readers and writers and new members of the "literacy club."

Many children have hundreds of hours of literacy interactions at home during which they develop understandings critical to their success in beginning reading. Our school programs must be structured to try to provide those experiences and interactions (that some children have already had) for all children. This will not be an easy task. Schools do not have the luxury of providing these learning experiences one-child-at-a-time, but teachers can offer literacy learning in ways that simulate these home experiences as closely as possible.

Critical Understandings That Are the Building Blocks to Success

The multilevel reading and writing activities presented in this book are the building blocks to success for ALL kindergarten children. When understood and applied in the classroom, these critical understandings will be observed in young learners:

1. Children learn that reading provides both enjoyment and information, and they develop the desire to learn to read and write.

2. Students also learn many new concepts and add words and meanings to their speaking vocabulary.

3. Children learn print concepts, including how to read words from left to right, to read a page from top to bottom, etc.

4. Children develop phonemic awareness, including the concept of rhyme.

5. Students learn to read and write some interesting-to-them words, like Pizza Hut® and cat.

6. Students learn some letter names and sounds usually connected to the interesting words they have learned.

In developmentally appropriate kindergartens, teachers provide a variety of experiences so that all children develop these critical understandings which are the building blocks to success!

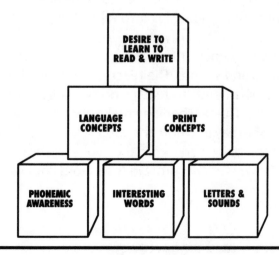

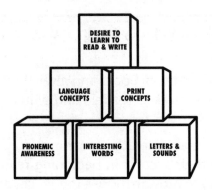

Chapter 11
Any Questions?

Frequently Asked Questions

1. Do you use a Word Wall in kindergarten?

"No, but our classrooms are "print-rich environments.""

The best Word Wall for a kindergarten class is a print-rich environment! In our kindergarten classes, there is print everywhere! The morning message, predictable charts, color words, number words, days of the week, months of the year, names, Writing Center picture dictionary words, science and social studies theme words, and environmental print are displayed and used. There is never a time in kindergarten when students have to recognize and spell words correctly using the Word Wall, as they do in first grade. Some kindergarten teachers like to put their students' names on a word wall, along with high frequency words they teach and work with daily. It is important to put up the names and words after you teach them, and not before! All print in a kindergarten classroom must have meaning to the students and must be part of the instructional program if students are to remember it when they go to first grade after the summer holidays.

2. What about letter-of-the-week type programs?

"The time spent on many skills and drills can be much more useful, meaningful, and fun if teachers work with letters and sounds all day long in their kindergarten classrooms."

Building Blocks teachers read several alphabet books weekly and integrate letter-sound activities into all of their activities. Letters and sounds are taught continuously, and it does not take 26 weeks to cover all the letters. During journal writing, the students demonstrate what they know about letters and sounds. The teacher monitors the students' writing and learns what she needs to teach, and who needs more coaching on letters and sounds. The teacher may make anecdotal notes about her students' writing. She may also note the various stages of spelling development she sees in their daily work. From these observations, the teacher plans lessons to help her students grow in their word knowledge.

Kindergarten teachers teach about letters and letter sounds when they write predictable charts, morning messages, do shared reading with big books, and during student writing. What is the best assessment to determine what your students know about letters and sounds? The best assessment is their daily journal writing. This is an uncoached writing time and teachers can assess their students' letter/sound knowledge and application on the spot. Teachers then know what sounds to work on and what letters and sounds to review.

The basis for all work with letters and sounds can come from the "Getting to Know You" activity done with the student's names (see Chapters 6 and 10). We find this to be an enjoyable way to teach as well as being very beneficial to the students.

3. Do you edit spelling before publishing students' books and stories?

"Absolutely not!"

Invented spelling enables kindergarten students to write about things that are important to them. The students write interesting words and create stories on various topics. If a teacher edits kindergarten spelling, many students can no longer read the text. It also sends a message to kindergarten students that they did their writing incorrectly. After working so hard on a particular piece, this can be a self-esteem deflator. If correct spelling becomes an issue, the students will begin to limit their vocabulary to words they can spell. The editing process is part of the first grade Four-Blocks program. Be a cheerleader, not an editor, in kindergarten! **And remember…invented spelling is phonics in use!**

4. How do you get it all done in kindergarten?

"It takes a lot of planning, integrating, and eliminating the 'fluff!'"

Building Blocks teachers have eliminated activities from their daily instruction that are only skill and drill. We avoid a lot of coloring activities and mindless worksheets. We model correct letter formation and use good handwriting in our daily work without using a formal handwriting program. We also avoid lavish art projects that involve more "teacher work" than student input. Our instruction reflects the best practices for all kinds of students. We do not work with only the most capable students!

5. Do you use lined paper in kindergarten?

"No. It is not developmentally appropriate for all students."

Kindergarten students need to write on unlined paper in their journals and at other times so that they can focus on content or what they are saying instead of concentrating on staying on the lines. Most kindergarten students are not developmentally ready for lined paper. Fine motor skills are not usually developed by five, but they are by seven. The writing center is the place to have a variety of writing tools and paper for experimentation. All assigned writing work needs to be on unlined paper.

6. Do you begin journal writing early in the school year?

"No, we show the students what writing is before we expect them to write in kindergarten."

Children need to see the teacher write and know what they are suppose to do and how to do it before they are expected to write. Watching the teacher write morning messages and predictable charts prepares kindergarten students for "real" writing later in the year.

7. Do you have centers in Building Blocks?

"Yes!!! Centers are a must in any kindergarten classroom."

Centers are an integral part of our day and we allow 60-75 minutes for them each day. During the first quarter, we also include extra time in the schedule for morning centers and enrichment. Our centers reflect teacher-guided activities that integrate the curriculum's themes, as well as providing many opportunities for student choices. Our centers include: sand and water tables, easel painting, blocks, computer, listening, reading, play dough, writing, art, science, social studies, math, puzzles, games, Read the Room center, housekeeping, grocery store, and Legos™. In January, the teacher begins to coach writing at the Writing Center and works with students individually for 10-15 minutes at a time.

8. What can I do with predictable charts instead of only "I Like_____."?

"Lots and lots!"

"I like_____." is just one easy chart to start with. Predictable charts can be used to discuss a good book or story (The best part was _____. My favorite character was _____.) Predictable charts can follow up on themes, units of studies, or a field trip (I saw a _____. My favorite color is _____. I learned that _____.) The ideas and learning are endless with predictable charts. We could write a whole book on the topic, and we have seen enough good ideas for predictable charts to be used every week of the year and more!

Professional References

Adams, Marilyn Jager (1991) *Beginning to Read: Thinking and Learning about Print.* Cambridge, MA: MIT Press.

Anderson, R. C., et al. (1985) *Becoming a Nation of Readers: The Report on the Commission on Reading.* Washington, DC: National Institute of Education.

Cullinan, Bernice (1992) *Read to Me: Raising Kids Who Love to Read.* New York: Scholastic, Inc.

Cunningham, P. M. & Allington, R. L. (1999) *Classrooms That Work: All Children Can Learn to Read and Write: 2nd ed.* New York: Addison, Wesley Longman.

Cunningham, P.M. & Hall, D.P. (1996) *Building Blocks: A Framework for Reading and Writing in Kindergartens That Work.* (Video) Clemmons, NC: Windward Productions.

Cunningham, P. M. & Hall, D. P. (1994) *Making Words.* Carthage, IL: Good Apple.

Cunningham, P.M., Hall, D.P., and Defee, M. "Nonability Grouped, Multilevel Multimethod Instruction: A Year in a First Grade Classroom," *Reading Teacher,* April 1991.

Cunningham, P.M., Hall, D.P., and Defee, M. "Multilevel Multimethod Instruction: Eight Years Later," *Reading Teacher,* May 1998.

Cunningham, P. M., Hall, D. P., and Sigmon, C. M. (1999) *The Teacher's Guide to the Four-Blocks™.* Greensboro, NC: Carson-Dellosa.

Fitzpatrick, Jo (1997) *Phonemic Awareness: Playing with Sounds to Strengthen Beginning Reading Skills.* Huntington Beach, CA: Creative Teaching Press.

Fulghum, Robert (1999) *All I Really Needed to Know I Learned in Kindergarten.* Topeka, KS: Econo-Clad Books.

Gentry, J. R. "You Can Analyze Developmental Spelling—And Here's How To Do It!" *Early Years K-8,* May 1985.

Gentry, J. R. & Gillet, J. W. (1993) *Teaching Kids to Spell.* Portsmouth, NH: Heinemann.

Gentry, J. R. (1987) *Spel is a Four Letter Word.* Portsmouth, NH: Heinemann.

Hall, D. P. & Cunningham, P.M. (1997) *Month-by-Month Reading and Writing in Kindergarten.* Greensboro, NC: Carson-Dellosa.

Jenkins, Karen S. (1997) *Kinder Krunchies: Healthy Snack Recipes for Children.* Discovery Toys, Inc.

Jordano, J. K. & Callella-Jones, Trisha (1998) *Winter Phonemic Awareness: Songs and Rhymes.* Huntington Beach, CA: Creative Teaching Press.

Jordano, J. K. & Callella-Jones, Trisha (1998) *Fall Phonemic Awareness: Songs and Rhymes.* Huntington Beach, CA: Creative Teaching Press.

Jordano, J. K. & Callella-Jones, Trisha (1998) *Spring Phonemic Awareness: Songs and Rhymes.* Huntington Beach, CA: Creative Teaching Press.

Morris, Darrell (1999) Paper presented at National Reading Conference, Orlando, FL.

Opitz, M. F. "Children's Books to Develop Phonemic Awareness—For You and Parents, Too!" *Reading Teacher* 51, no. 6 (1998).

Read, C. "Children's Categorizations of Speech Sounds in English." *National Council of Teachers of English Research Report* no. 17 (1975).

Richels, Donald J. "Understanding and Supporting Children's Invented Spelling." Northern Illinois University.

Routman, Regie (1996) *Literacy at the Crossroads: Crucial Talk about Reading, Writing, and Other Teaching Dilemmas.* Portsmouth, NH: Heinemann.

Schlosser, Kristen & Phillips, Vicki (1994) *Building Interactive Charts.* New York: Scholastic Trade.

Sulzby, Elizabeth & Teale, William (1991) "Emergent Literacy." *Handbook of Reading Research Volume II.* Edited by R. Barr et al. New York: Longman Publishing.

Trealease, Jim (1987) *The Read-Aloud Handbook.* New York: Penguin Books.

Yopp, Hallie Kay "Developing Phonemic Awareness" *Reading Teacher* 45, no. 9 (1992).

Children's Materials Cited:

A Busy Year by Leo Lionni (Alfred Knopf, 1969).

A Hunting We Will Go by Steven Kellogg (Morrow Jr. Books, 1998).

A is for Animals: 26 Pop-Up Surprises by David Pelham (Simon & Schuster, 1991).

A You're Adorable by Buddy Kaye, Fred Wise, and Sidney Lippman (Candlewick Press, 1994).

ABC I Like Me! by Nancy Carlson (Viking Children's Books, 1997).

Accidental Zucchini: An Unexpected Alphabet by Max Grover (Harcourt Brace & Co., 1996).

Alexander and the Terrible, Horrible, No Good, Very Bad Day by Judith Viorst (Atheneum, 1972).

Alexander the Wind Up Mouse by Leo Lionni (Alfred Knopf, 1991).

Alice in Wonderland (Dover Children's Thrift Classics) by Lewis Carroll (Dover Publishing, 1999).

Alicia Has a Bad Day by Lisa Jahn-Clough (Houghton Mifflin Co., 1994).

Alphababies by Kim Golding (DK Publishing, Inc., 1998).

Arf! Beg! Catch! Dogs from A to Z by Henry Horenstein (Scholastic, Inc., 1999).

Arthur Babysits by Marc Brown (Little, Brown & Co., 1992).

Arthur's Birthday by Marc Brown (Little, Brown & Co., 1989).

Arthur's Family Vacation by Marc Brown (Little, Brown & Co., 1993).

Arthur's First Sleepover by Marc Brown (Little, Brown & Co., 1994).

Arthur's Neighborhood by Marc Brown (Random House, 1996).

Arthur's New Puppy by Marc Brown (Little, Brown & Co., 1993).

Arthur's Pet Business by Marc Brown (Little, Brown & Co., 1990).

Arthur's Teacher Trouble by Marc Brown (Little, Brown & Co., 1986).

Arthur's Tooth by Marc Brown (Little, Brown & Co., 1985).

Arthur's TV Troubles by Marc Brown (Little, Brown & Co., 1995).

Arthur Writes a Story by Marc Brown (Little, Brown & Co., 1996).

Bats by Gail Gibbons (Holiday House, Inc., 1999).

The Bat Jamboree by Kathi Appelt (William Morrow & Co., 1996).

Bear in a Square by Stella Blockstone (Scholastic, Inc., 1998).

Bearsie Bear and the Surprise Sleepover Party by Bernard Waber (Houghton Mifflin Co., 1997).

Big Anthony and the Magic Ring by Tomie dePaola (Harcourt Brace & Co., 1979).

The Biggest House in the World by Leo Lionni (Alfred Knopf, 1968).

Blueberries for Sal by Robert McCloskey (Viking Press, 1987).

Boats by Byron Barton (HarperCollins Children's Books, 1986).

Brave Irene by William Steig (Farrar, Straus & Giroux, 1986).

Bringing the Rain to Kapiti Plain by Verna Aardema (Scholastic, Inc., 1981).

Brown Bear, Brown Bear, What Do You See? by Bill Martin, Jr. (Holt, Rinehart & Winston, 1970).

The Carrot Seed by Ruth Krauss & Crockett Johnson (HarperCollins Children's Books, 1988).

Cats by Gail Gibbons (Holiday House, Inc., 1998).

Chicka Chicka Boom Boom by Bill Martin, Jr. & John Archambault (Simon & Schuster, Inc., 1989).

Cinderella by Alan Trussell-Cullen (Dominie, 1999).

Clifford Gets a Job by Norman Bridwell (Scholastic, Inc., 1965).

Clifford the Big Red Dog by Norman Bridwell (Scholastic, Inc., 1983).

Clifford's ABC by Norman Bridwell (Scholastic, Inc., 1983).

Clifford's Good Deeds by Norman Bridwell (Scholastic, Inc., 1985).

Clifford's Puppy Days by Norman Bridwell (Scholastic, Inc., 1989).

The Cloud Book by Tomie dePaola (Holiday House, Inc., 1975).

Color Dance by Ann Jonas (Greenwillow Books, 1989).

Colors at the Zoo by Phoebe Henderson (William H. Sadlier, Inc., 1998).

Corduroy's Christmas by B. G. Hennessy (Scholastic, Inc., 1992).

The Crayon Counting Book by Pam Munoz Ryan & Jerry Pallotta (Cambridge, 1996).

Dealing with Addition by Lynette Long (Charlesbridge Publishing, 1998).

Dinner at Aunt Connie's House by Faith Ringgold (Hyperion, 1998).

Do You Want to Be My Friend? by Eric Carle (HarperCollins Children's Books, 1971).

The Doorbell Rang (Big Book) by Pat Hutchins (Scholastic Big Books, 1986).

The Doorbell Rang by Pat Hutchins (William Morrow & Co., 1992).

Dr. DeSoto by William Steig (Farrar, Straus & Giroux, 1982).

Dr. DeSoto Goes to Africa by William Steig (HarperCollins Children's Books, 1992).

Eating Fractions by Bruce McMillan (Scholastic Trade, 1991).

Eating the Alphabet: Fruits and Vegetables from A to Z by Lois Ehlert (Voyager Books, 1989).

The First Dog by Jan Brett (Harcourt Brace & Co., 1992).

The First Thanksgiving by Linda Hayward (Econo-Clad Books, 1999).

Fish Eyes: A Book You Can Count On by Lois Ehlert (Harcourt Brace & Company, 1990).

Five Little Monkeys Jumping on the Bed by Eileen Christelow (Houghton Mifflin Co., 1989).

Flossie and the Fox by Patricia C. McKissack (Dial Books, 1986).

Fraction Fun by David Adler (Holiday House, Inc., 1996).

Franklin and the Thunderstorm by Paulette Bourgeois (Scholastic, Inc., 1998).

Franklin Goes to School by Paulette Bourgeois (Scholastic Trade, 1995).

Franklin in the Dark by Paulette Bourgeois (Scholastic, Inc., 1986).

Franklin Is Bossy by Paulette Bourgeois (Scholastic, Inc., 1993).

Franklin Is Lost by Paulette Bourgeois (Scholastic, Inc., 1992).

Franklin's New Friend by Paulette Bourgeois (Scholastic, Inc., 1997).

Frederick by Leo Lionni (Alfred Knopf, 1967).

Freight Train by Donald Crews (Beech Tree Books, 1996).

Frog and Toad Are Friends by Arnold Lobel (HarperCollins Children's Books, 1987).

The Frog Prince by Alan Trussell-Cullen (Dominie, 1999).

Frogs Jump: A Counting Book by Alan Brooks (Scholastic, Inc., 1996).

Frogs by Kevin J. Holmes (Capstone Press, 1999).

Frogs by Michael Tyler (Mondo, 1997).

The Gingerbread Baby by Jan Brett (G. P. Putnam, 1997).

The Gingerbread Boy by Paul Galdone (Houghton Mifflin Co., 1983).

The Gingerbread Boy by Alan Trussell-Cullen (Dominie, 1999).

Golden Bear (Big Book) by Ruth Young (Houghton Mifflin Co., 1996).

Golden Bear by Ruth Young (Penguin Books, 1992).

Good Night! by Claire Masurel and Muriel Henry (Chronical Books, 1993).

Good Night, Moon by Margaret Wise Brown (Scholastic, Inc., 1989).

The Great Golden Easter Egg Hunt by Liza Baker (Scholastic, Inc., 2000).

Gregory, the Terrible Eater by Mitchell Sharmat (Simon & Schuster, 1980).

The Grouchy Ladybug (HarperCollins Children's Books, 1996).

Growing Vegetable Soup by Lois Ehlert (Voyager Books, 1987).

The Hat by Jan Brett (G. P. Putnam, 1997).

I Have a Dream by Martin Luther King, Jr., (Scholastic, Inc., 1997).

I Know an Old Lady Who Swallowed a Fly by Nadine Bernard Westcott (Little, Brown & Co., 1980).

I Went Walking by Susan Williams (Harcourt Brace & Co., 1989).

If a Bus Could Talk: The Story of Rosa Parks by Faith Ringgold (Simon & Schuster, 1999).

If You Give a Mouse a Cookie by Laura Joffe Numeroff (HarperCollins Children's Books, 1999).

Ira Sleeps Over by Bernard Waber (Houghton Mifflin Co., 1973).

The Island of the Skog by Steven Kellogg (Puffin, 1983).

It's a Fruit, It's a Vegetable, It's a Pumpkin by Allan Fowler (Children's Press, 1995).

It's a Perfect Day by Abigail Pizer (Scott Foresman, 1990).

It's Pumpkin Time by Zoe Hall (Scholastic, Inc., 1994).

Jack and the Beanstalk by Steven Kellogg (Mulberry Books, 1997).

Jamie O'Rourke and the Big Potato by Tomie dePaola (Penguin Putnam, 1992).

Johnny Appleseed by Steven Kellogg (Scholastic, Inc., 1988).

The Jolly Postman by Janet and Allen Ahlberg (Little, Brown & Co., 1986).

Just Graph It! by Sandi Hill (Creative Teaching Press, 1980).

K Is for Kiss Goodnight: A Bedtime Alphabet by Jill Sardegna (Delacorte Press, 1994).

The Lap-Time Song and Play Book by Margot Tomes (Harcourt Brace & Co., 1989).

Learning Basic Skills through Music, Vol. 1 by Hap Palmer (Kimbo Educational Audio, 1988).

The Little Red Hen by Paul Galdone (Houghton Mifflin Co., 1985).

Louie's Goose by H. M. Ehrlich (Houghton Mifflin Co., 2000).

The M & M's Brand Counting Book by Barbara Barbieri McGrath (Charlesbridge, 1994).

Make Way for Ducklings by Robert McCloskey (Viking, 1942).

Meow! by Katya Arnold (Holiday House, Inc., 1998).

Mike Mulligan and His Steam Shovel by Virginia Lee Burton (Houghton Mifflin Co., 1978).

Miss Bindergarten Gets Ready for Kindergarten by Joseph Slate (Dutton Books, 1996).

Miss Bindergarten's Hundredth Day of Kindergarten by Joseph Slate (Dutton Books, 1998).

Miss Spider's Tea Party by David Kirk (Scholastic, Inc., 1994).

The Mitten by Jan Brett (G. P. Putnam, 1989).

The Mixed-Up Chameleon by Eric Carle (HarperCollins Children's Books, 1987).

Monkey-Monkey's Trick: Based on an African Folktale by Patricia McKissack (Random House, 1988).

Moonbear's Books by Frank Asch (Houghton Mifflin Co., 1996).

Mouse Mess by Linnea Riley (Scholastic, Inc., 1997).

Mr. Rabbit and the Lovely Present by Charlotte Zolotow (HarperCollins Juvenille Books, 1990).

Mrs. Wishy Washy by Joy Crowley (Rigby Big Books, 1983).

Mufaro's Beautiful Daughters by John Steptoe (Scholastic, Inc., 1987).

My Friend the Gorilla by Atsuko Morozumi (Farrar, Straus & Giroux, 1997).

My Little Sister Ate One Hare by Bill Grossman (Crown Publishers, 1996).

The Mysterious Tadpole by Steven Kellogg (Puffin Books, 1977).

Nests, Nests, Nests by Susan Canizares and Mary Reid (Scholastic Trade, 1998).

Old MacDonald Had a Farm: The Traditional Nursery Song by Prue Theobalds (Peter Bedrick, 1991).

Once There Were Twelve by Metro, 1999

One of Each by Mary Ann Hoberman (Scholastic, Inc., 1997).

One Watermelon Seed by Celia Barker Lottridge (Oxford University Press, 1986).

Our Granny by Margaret Wild (Houghton Mifflin Co., 1994).

Over in the Meadow by John Langstaff (Harcourt Brace & Co., 1957).

Paddington's ABC by Michael Bond (Viking Books, 1991).

A Picture Book of Abraham Lincoln by David Adler (Holiday House, Inc., 1989).

A Picture Book of George Washington by David Adler (Holiday House, Inc., 1989).

A Picture Book of Martin Luther King, Jr. by David Adler (Holiday House, Inc., 1989).

A Picture Book of Rosa Parks by David Adler (Holiday House, Inc., 1993).

Pigs by Gail Gibbons (Holiday House, Inc., 1999).

Planes by Anne Rockwell (Dutton, 1985).

Polar Express by Chris Van Allsburg (Houghton Mifflin Co., 1985).

The Princess and the Pea by Alan Trussell-Cullen (Dominie, 1999).

The Pumpkin Book by Gail Gibbons (Scholastic, Inc., 1999).

Pumpkin Pumpkin by Jeanne Titherington (William Morrow & Co., 1986).

Purple, Green, and Yellow by Robert Munch (Annick Press, 1992).

The Quilt Story by Tony Johnson (The Putnam Publishing Group, 1985).

Rabbits, Rabbits, and More Rabbits by Gail Gibbons (Holiday House, Inc., 2000).

The Rainbow Fish by Marcus Pfister (North South Books, 1996).

The Relatives Came by Cynthia Rylant (Aladdin Books, 1985).

Rooster's Off to See the World by Eric Carle (Simon & Schuster, 1987).

Santa's Favorite Story by Hisako Aoki (Scholastic, Inc., 1991).

Sea Squares by Joy N. Hulme (Hyperion Books, 1991).

Side By Side by Lee Bennett Hopkins (Simon & Schuster, 1988).

Silver Packages: An Appalachian Christmas Story by Cynthia Rylant (Orchard Books, 1997).

Skip to My Lou by Nadine Bernard Westcott (Little, Brown & Co., 1989).

Spiders by Gail Gibbons (Holiday House, Inc.,1993).

Stellaluna by Janell Cannon (Scholastic, Inc., 1993).

The Story of Ruby Bridges by Robert Coles (Scholastic, Inc., 1995).

Strega Nona by Tomie dePaola (Simon & Schuster, 1975).

Strega Nona's Magic Lessons by Tomie dePaola (Harcourt Brace & Co., 1982).

Swimmy by Leo Lionni (Random House, 1963).

Sylvester and the Magic Pebbles by William Steig (Simon & Schuster, 1969).

Tar Beach by Faith Ringgold (Crowne, 1991).

Thank You, Santa by Margaret Wild (Scholastic, Inc., 1991).

Things I Like by Anthony Browne (Houghton Mifflin Co., 1994).

This Is the Way by Anne Dalton (Scholastic, Inc., 1992).

This Old Man by Carol Jones (Houghton Mifflin Co., 1990).

Three Billy Goats Gruff by Allan Trusell-Cullen (Dominie, 1999).

The Three Little Pigs by Eileen Grace (Troll Associates, 1981).

The Three Little Pigs by Alan Trussell-Cullen (Dominie, 1999).

To Market, To Market by Anne Miranda (Scholastic, Inc., 1997).

Tom Goes to Kindergarten by Margaret Wild (Albert Whitman and Co., 1999).

The Town Mouse and the Country Mouse by Helen Craig (Candlewick Press, 1992).

Trouble With Trolls by Jan Brett (Puffin Books, 1992).

Truck Jam by Paul Strickland (Rugged Bears Publishing Co./Discovery Toys, 1999).

Trucks by Byron Barton (HarperCollins, 1986).

Trucks You Can Count On by Doug Magee (The Putnam Publishing Group, 1985).

Tucking Mommy In in the Morning by Morang Loh (Orchard Books, 1987).

The Very Busy Spider by Eric Carle (Philomel Books, 1985).

The Very Clumsy Click Beetle by Eric Carle (Philomel Books, 1999).

The Very Hungry Caterpillar by Eric Carle (The Putnam Publishing Group, 1984).

The Very Quiet Cricket by Eric Carle (The Putnam Publishing Group, 1997).

What Can Rabbit Hear? by Lucy Cousins (Tambourine Books, 1991).

What Will Mommy Do When I'm at School? by Delores Johnson (Aladdin Books, 1998).

What Will the Weather Be Like Today? by Paul Rogers (Scholastic, Inc., 1989).

When I Feel Angry by Cornelia Maude Spelman (Albert Whitman and Co., 2000).

Where the Wild Things Are by Maurice Sendak (HarperCollins Children's Books, 1988).

Where's Spot? by Eric Hill (The Putnam Publishing Group, 1980).

White Rabbit's Color Book by Alan Baker (Kingfisher Books, 1994).

Who Said Red by Mary Serfozo (Econo-Clad Books, 1999).

The Wimp by Kathy Caple (Houghton Mifflin Co., 2000).

Wonderful Worms by Linda Glaser (The Millbrook Press, 1992).

The Year of the Perfect Christmas Tree by Gloria Houston (Dial Books, 1985).

Zeke Peppin by William Steig (HarperCollins, 1994).

Zipping, Zapping, Zooming Bats by Ann Earle (HarperCollins, 1995).

Zoo-Looking by Mem Fox (Mondo, 1996).

Additional References:

Hayner, Emilie. "Helping Your Children Learn to Read: Understanding Phonemic Awareness."
    (Reproducible)

A WORD FROM YOUR CHILD'S TEACHER

Helping Your Child Learn to Read: Understanding PHONEMIC AWARENESS

We used to think that there were certain skills that children needed to develop before they could learn to read. Before teaching them to read, we would give them tests to assess whether or not they were ready to read. We would ask them to name letters, match pictures with their beginning sounds, find objects which look alike, and we would measure their understanding of vocabulary and use of oral language. With these "reading readiness" tests, we would determine which children were ready to begin formal reading instruction, and which ones needed more time to develop readiness.

In the last 15 years, our understanding of the way children learn to read has shifted from "reading readiness" to a new concept known as "emergent literacy," or "preliteracy." We now know that literacy develops gradually through a variety of experiences with reading and writing, beginning at birth. As children are reading books and other print around them (signs, advertisements, products in the grocery store, etc.) they begin to:

- understand why we read and write

- build background knowledge

- learn print concepts (i.e., we read from left to right and top to bottom

- learn some concrete words

- learn some letter names and sounds

- develop a desire to learn to read and write on their own

Literacy literally **emerges** in their young minds as each of these understandings develops.

One of the crucial aspects of literacy that develops in emergent readers is known as **phonemic awareness**.

What is phonemic awareness?

In the most basic sense, phonemic awareness is the recognition that words are made up of individual sounds and the ability to manipulate sounds. Phonemic awareness develops through a series of stages during which children understand that language is made up of words, which, in turn, are made up of syllables, which are made up of phonemes (or individual sounds). Phonemic awareness is an oral ability, enabling children to identify rhyming words and words that begin the same. Children that have phonemic awareness can also hear individual sounds in a word (i.e., three sounds in the word d-o-g) and say these sounds separately.

Children enter school at many different stages of emergent literacy, with different levels of phonemic awareness, but all need to progress through each level before they become fluent readers. As parents, you have and will continue to play a large role in your child's literacy.

How do we assess phonemic awareness?

Children who have developed phonemic awareness understand rhyme, beginning word sounds, and sounds within words. As you read to and talk with your child, ask her which words start with the same sound. One thing to keep in mind is that children first recognize similar sounds in words that are meaningful to them, such as *Mommy, McDonald's®, Daddy,* and *dog.* When you read your child nursery rhymes, leave out the last rhyming word in each line so she can "fill in the blank." If these tasks come easily to your child, she is well on the way to phonemic awareness. If she has some difficulty (which is very normal at this age), don't worry—it will come. In either case, there are many ways you can help your child become more phonemically aware.

How can you help your child develop phonemic awareness?

First of all, read, read, and read some more! When your child hears you read, she hears the sounds that make up the words, and begins to develop phonemic awareness. This is true when you read anything to your child, although some things will develop phonemic awareness more effectively than others.

The Teacher's Guide to Building Blocks

Alphabet books are an excellent resource for phonemic awareness, as they emphasize the beginning sounds of words. When you read these books, ask your child to name the objects he sees in the pictures, and stress those first letter sounds. You might throw in some words that your child knows well as the letter comes up, such as his name ("M is for mouse, and for Matthew!"), names of his siblings or pets, or names of his favorite toys or restaurants. Words that are meaningful to children are more likely to be remembered and stored away for future reference than those with which they have no connection. Point out words that you see as you drive, and ask your child to tell you other words that start the same way. You will be amazed at how much your child can learn about words from simple activities like this.

Nursery rhymes and *Dr. Seuss* books are also great sources for phonemic awareness development. The rhythm and rhyme of books like these make them easy to remember and fun to recite. When you read books written in rhyme ask your child to help you finish each phrase with the rhyming word. Sing or recite nursery rhymes with your child as you play together or set the table. As your child learns the nursery rhymes, write them down and "read" them with her. Nothing is more encouraging to a child than the feeling that she can actually read something. Play rhyming games, allowing your child to make up words if he can't think of real words, as long as they rhyme. Dr. Seuss was a master at playing with words like this. You and your child will both appreciate Seuss's ability with words in books like *There's a Wocket in My Pocket* (Random House, 1974). We do many of these activities in our classroom to encourage phonemic awareness. As you may have already guessed, we have a good time playing with words and listening for specific sounds. We also spend time clapping along with words, taking notice of the syllables within words. At home, you may want to ask your child to clap her name for you. Even though she may not understand the word "syllable," you will see that she can apply the principle and tell you how many beats she hears in the word. As children become more adept at this activity, they can tell the difference between short words and long words, which will help them as they begin to read short and long words on a page.

Great Books That Encourage Phonemic Awareness

Alphabet Books:
- *A, My Name is Alice* by Jane Bayer (NAL/Dutton, 1987).
- *A is for…?* by Henry Horenstein (Harcourt Brace & Co., 1999).
- *A is for Artist* by Christopher Hudson (The J. Paul Getty Museum, 1997).
- *Basketball ABC* by Florence Cassen Mayers (Harry N. Abrams, Inc., 1996).

Rhyming Books:
Anything by Dr. Seuss! Some favorites are:
- *There's a Wocket in My Pocket* (Random House, 1974).
- *One Fish, Two Fish, Red Fish, Blue Fish* (Random House, 1960).
- *Horton Hears a Who!* (Random House, 1976).

You may also enjoy:
- *Brown Bear, Brown Bear, What Do You See?* by Eric Carle (Henry Holt & Co., 1983).
- *Tomie de Paola's Favorite Nursery Tales* by Tomie de Paola (Putnam, 1986).
- *Tumble Bumble* by Felicia Bond (Front Street, 1996).
- *Miss Spider's Tea Party* by David Kirk (Scholastic, Inc., 1997).
- *My Nose Is a Hose* by Ken Salisbury (McClanahan Books, 1997).

For help in finding children's literature:
- Database of Award-Winning Children's Literature www2.wcoil.com/~ellerbee/childlit.html
- The Randolph Caldecott Medal www.ala.org/alsc/caldecott.html

I love helping children develop literacy, and am excited to have your children in my class this year. Thank you for all you do to encourage your child's progress in learning. I hope that you will be constantly amazed and surprised by the things your child comes up with as he or she develops phonemic awareness and begins to read. This is an exciting time of life for our children! Enjoy each day and the learning that it brings.